GROW YOUR OWN
FAMILY TREE

A Comprehensive Guide
To
Tracing Your Ancestry

Pauline Golds

Emerald Guides

© Pauline Golds 2016-First Edition

ISBN
978-1-84716-602-9

Printed by 4edge www.4edge.co.uk

Cover design by Pauline Golds/Bookworks Islington

Original images by Mikey Jackson www.mikeyjackson.com

This Book is Dedicated to my Family

Those who have long since passed into the Silent Land, those who have travelled beside me along the way and those who are yet to begin the journey.

Contents

Preface

About ten years ago when I found myself hurtling toward the grand old age of fifty, I began, for the first time, to feel mortal. It was about this time that the BBC series "Who Do You Think You Are?" was first aired and one of the first celebrities to participate was the actress Amanda Redman, who had been in my class at school. This got me thinking about my own ancestors. I realised that I didn't even know the Christian names of my grandparents or my grandmothers' maiden names! Fortunately for me, the wonderful World Wide Web had now taken a firm foothold and it was possible to find these things out. Unfortunately for me, my parents had both passed away and I had lost all contact with elderly aunts and uncles, so I didn't have much of a starting point.

However, with patience and determination over the next couple of years I spent a lot of my spare time delving into that strange country they call the past, or at least the areas of it that were graced by my ancestors.

I discovered chimney sweeps and gamekeepers, blacksmiths and agricultural labourers, fishmongers and midwives to name but a few. I uncovered dark secrets of illegitimacy and crime and sad tales of poverty and the workhouse. I suppose when I began I was hoping to find I was descended from an Earl or a famous scientist, perhaps even a renowned actress, but it wasn't to be. Like the majority of people from Britain's past, my ancestors were working class. They were poor, illiterate and they often met with disease and early death. I think by learning all this, not only did it connect me to my ancestors, it also made me thankful that I was born in the second half of the 20th century and did not have to endure the hardships of the past.

Since tracing my own family tree (and it is an ongoing project as more and more resources become available), I have had the pleasure of discovering the ancestors of friends and extended family, many of whom said to me "You should do this for a living!" So I did and the rest is history.

I now want to help others on their own voyage into the past. Hiring a professional is not always an option, but with time and patience and a few tips on the dos and don'ts, it *is* possible to Grow Your Own Family Tree.

In this book I will stick to what I know best, that is the British Isles. With all its variations in language, culture and class it is as fascinating a journey as anywhere in the world.

Good Luck and I hope your journey is as exciting and enlightening as mine.

Pauline Golds
2016

Chapter 1 – What Resources are Available?

1 – Begin at the Beginning

Many people think that the first place to start researching your family tree is by visiting some dusty old archive or by logging on to the internet. WRONG.

Your research should begin at home, firstly with yourself. You may think that the knowledge you already have is all there is, but might there be some old documents you have inherited lying in the back of a drawer somewhere? What about old photographs? Perhaps you have seen photographs in old albums and not known who they are, but perhaps if you take them out of the album, some thoughtful ancestor might have written a name or even a date on the back.

Whilst we are on this subject, this is a must for all those who want to pass on information to future generations. When you have a spare moment go through all your photographs and write names and dates on the back. This could prove invaluable to those trying to trace *you* some day.

Anyway, I digress. After you have exhausted all possible avenues of research in your own home, then is the time to contact all the relatives. Older generations are particularly useful, but siblings, cousins and even nieces and nephews may hold some key information that they have either as documents or as memories of tales long past told to them. Once you have gathered everything you possibly can, then it's time to move on.

One more word of advice here, always work methodically. Start with one surname and if possible continue with that line until you have exhausted all your options. Then move on to the next surname, working chronologically back in time.

2 – The Internet

Most people nowadays have a home computer, but if you don't have access to one then it's not always a problem. Many libraries offer online access. Often this is free and they usually give assistance to those who are novices in IT.

There is a huge amount of information online now and that information is growing all the time. However, with so much around it can be daunting knowing where to begin. Most websites charge a subscription or a 'pay as you go' method and the costs can mount up if you don't use them wisely.

I have 2 personal favourites that I have ongoing subscriptions with: ancestry.co.uk and findmypast.co.uk. (From hereon I shall refer to these sites as 'Ancestry' and 'Find my Past'). These sites offer a range of payment options. Most websites, including these 2, offer a free trial for a limited time and this is the best way to start. If you like what you find, then it is probably best to begin with a monthly subscription (if this is an option), and once you are certain you intend to proceed in your quest, upgrade to an annual if funds allow. It always works out cheaper in the long run to purchase the longer alternative.

Also it probably goes without saying that if you are not aware of any ancestors that hail from other countries, then just stick to the UK subscription if this is an option. Some websites such as the genealogist.co.uk offer different levels for subscription within the UK records. This can sometimes be frustrating because just as you think you have found something of interest, it tells you can access it only if you upgrade.

If a website offers a subscription, then it is almost always preferable to the 'pay as you go' alternative. At first these may seem better value, but you often find yourself paying for false leads. Subscriptions allow you unlimited access to the records, so no matter how many times you reach a dead end, at least you have only wasted a little time, not money. There are many very good websites that are free and it is well worth making full use of these.

I particularly recommend:

freereg.org.uk, freecen.org.uk, freebmd.org.uk and familysearch.org.

Sites that you pay for usually have a mixture of original document images and transcripts. The downside of free websites is that they are invariably only transcripts, not images of original documents. Most transcripts will be accurate copies of original documentation, but it must be remembered that they have been transcribed by human beings, often volunteers, and human beings are prone to occasional errors. Some documents are hundreds of years old and are faded, chewed by church mice and written in a hand very unlike our own, so even the most experienced transcriber can sometimes get it wrong.

Therefore, as far as possible always source your information from original documentation. You will find that the more often you look at the old and barely legible images, the more accustomed you will become to deciphering them. I suppose what I am trying to say here is, by all means use what others have done for you, but always double check where possible and trust your own judgement.

One very important word of warning here that I cannot emphasise enough is do not treat other people's research as written in stone. Many websites allow you to build your family tree and put it online for others to see. When I first began I often took names from these trees and it led me on many a wild goose chase. Many people rush in head first, see a name that looks a bit like what they want it to look like and add it to their tree. Always check this information for yourself. If you can't find it, then ask yourself "How did they find it?" Often you can contact the person though a message and ask them their source. My advice would be, if they don't answer, then disregard the information.

If looking for particular records such as apprenticeship or bastardy documents, a very useful website is genguide.co.uk which gives useful guides as to which resources offer what information.

Finally, occasionally it can be worth just typing an ancestor's name and possibly a few details directly into a search engine. This can be especially useful if your ancestor had an unusual name. My great x 2 grandfather's name was Cephas Tree and just by typing his name into Google I discovered a lead to a newspaper article outlining the story of when he and his daughter were condemned to hang for burglary. I was then able to find the original story in local newspapers in the East Sussex Records Office. (More about him in Chapter 7).

3 – Family History Societies

Most counties and/or areas have Family History Societies and Groups that can prove to be invaluable, but once again they vary greatly in their usefulness. Most charge a yearly subscription of between £10 and £15 and for that you usually get a quarterly magazine. What you get besides is where they differ. Some, like my own county Sussex, give free access to all pre 1837 baptisms and burials and a wide choice of CDs to purchase with other useful information such as marriages and monumental inscriptions. Others will look up information in their local archives either for free or for a fee. The key here is to look carefully into what they can offer you. If it is not totally clear on their website, email them to find out exactly what you can expect for your money.

If the Society you are interested in is close enough to you, you may be interested in local meetings and events that they hold. Here you can often pick up tips from others, both amateur and professional. Also they often arrange trips to local or National Archives and can help you with your research there. The Federation of Family History Societies may help you find the Society that could be most useful to you and provide you with other practical information. Their website is http://ffhs.org.uk A final note, if the Society is not in your area and you are just interested in obtaining baptism, marriage and burial records, don't forget that in some cases the information you need may all be available on the general websites, so always check them out first before you join up to a Society.

4 – Archives and Libraries

When I first began my quest to trace my family tree, I assumed as many people do, that my first port of call to find original parish records would be in the parishes themselves. I had an idea that I would be trekking around towns and villages, talking to the local clergymen and looking through dusty old documents that had been held in the same location for hundreds of years - WRONG.

Very few churches still keep their original records. They are mostly deposited in local archives and records offices. Many have been scanned and uploaded onto computers or at the very least have been copied onto microfilm or microfiche which are available to view when you visit.

Archives and other repositories hold a wealth of information that is not yet available on websites. The National Archives holds millions of records many of which can now be searched and even downloaded online. A visit to the County Records Office is also often very fruitful. However, it is always best to register with them first and check exactly what documents they hold. As you delve deeper into your family history, you will be looking for more personal details than just names and dates. Local resources are much more likely to hold what you are looking for.

County Records Offices almost always offer a look-up service for you which could save you travel costs. However, many of them charge a very high hourly rate with no guarantee of success, so be careful when considering using their services.

As well as County Archives there are many other repositories that hold useful information. I have found that sometimes County Libraries give a much more personal and cheaper online service. The rule is to always email or ring first to find out exactly what they can offer you. Sometimes the websites are a little ambiguous so if you are not sure – ask.

****

Chapter 2 – Birth, Marriage and Death – Part 1

1 – Getting Started

The first thing to do once you have gathered together all the documentation and noted memories of family members is to get organised.

Write down everything as you go, either in a Word document on the computer or on paper. Working on the computer is almost always preferable, because changes can be made and information added without the need for crossings out or rewrites. Printers are really cheap these days and well worth investing in if you don't already have one. (Do be aware though that ink is not usually cheap. In the course of my work I probably spend more on ink in a couple of months than I spent on my printer in the first place).

Most printers now come with a scanner which can also be very useful. I think it adds to the presentation of your research if photographs of your ancestors are included on the page that details their information. I also like to add old images of places where they lived to get a feel for their surroundings.

Once you are certain that you have all the information available, then print it out. Whichever way you decide to record your work, always keep it stored neatly in a folder, filed in order. Use subject dividers for each surname and place certificates and other documents in punched plastic wallets.

Always try to work on one ancestor at a time, working backwards through that line until you reach a dead end. (These dead ends are not always permanent. Periodically going back to previous research can sometimes offer new leads when fresh information becomes available).

It is important to always reference your sources. This is most easily done using footnotes. If doing this with Word, place your cursor next to the fact that you want referenced, then simply click on the "References" tab on the tool bar at the top of the page and then click on footnotes and add your reference.

It is most common for people to start their research with either their mother or their father. You probably know their date of birth, so this is the starting point. If you have their birth certificate it can supply you with information you may not know, such as their father's occupation or their mother's maiden name. Of course you may already know these facts and some, such as the father's occupation are interesting but not vital to further the research.

If you are really lucky, you will have information that occurred before 1911. This is when the last available census is viewable and this will be covered in the next chapter.

2 – Birth, Marriage and Death Certificates

The chances are though that you will not have this information, so obtaining birth certificates may be vital. Since 1837 in England and Wales (1855 in Scotland and 1864 in Ireland) it has been a legal requirement for every birth, marriage and death to be officially registered and certificates of proof issued. For England and Wales, these certificates are now available to order from the Government Record Office. (For Scotland and Ireland see the relevant chapter). There are several ways to find the certificate you wish to order. If you have not yet subscribed to any of the general websites, you should be able to find details at freebmd.org.uk. Simply type in as many details as you can e.g. name, year of birth, district of birth, and hit the 'find' button. One thing to mention here is that towns within the boundaries of registration districts vary over time and are sometimes quite surprising. If you are looking for a fairly common name it may be worth checking that you have the right district. This information is available on genuki.org.uk.

If you have already subscribed to a general website such as Ancestry or Find my Past, then these indexes are also available there. They will give you the information you need to order the certificate. That is the District, the Quarter of the year, the Volume no. and the Page no. Since September 1911 the mother's maiden name has also appeared in the index and this may be all you need to further your research. If this is the case then you may be able to avoid buying the certificate at least at this stage.

You may find that you have all the information you need from online parish records (see Chapter 4), but if you do need or want to purchase the certificate, do not fall into the trap of ordering it from one of the ancestry websites. It is much cheaper to order it directly from gro.gov.uk. At the time of writing, these certificates cost £9.25 each. You will need to register with the site then simply fill in the information and pay by debit or credit card.

The certificates take about a week to arrive and will give you the following information:

- The name, date and place of birth.
- The father's name (if a father is recorded) and occupation.
- The mother's name, maiden surname and, after 1984, occupation.
- After 1969 the parents' places of birth are also recorded.

Example of information on Birth Certificate

Once you have the birth certificate, it will give you all the information you need to order the parents' marriage certificate. The references can be found and the documents ordered in exactly the same way as before. Marriage certificates give you:

- The date and place of marriage.
- The name, age and marital status of the parties.
- Their occupation and address.
- The name and occupation of each party's father.
- The names of the witnesses.
- The name of the person who solemnised the marriage.

Example of information on Marriage Certificate

Death certificates, although not always necessary, can prove interesting reading . I tend to have a rather morbid curiosity as to what people died of, particularly if they died young.

Death certificates give you:

- The name, date and place of death.
- The date and place of birth (prior to1969 a certificate only showed the age of deceased).
- The occupation and usual address.
- The cause of death.
- The person who gave the information for the death registration.

Example of information on Death Certificate

Sometimes certificates give you surprising clues. For example, you may not be entirely sure that you have the right person, but perhaps the name of the witnesses are members of the same family or even neighbours (something you can check on the censuses). It can sometimes be frustrating when there are several possibilities in the indexes. On occasion you may need to buy more than one certificate before you get the right one. This is why it is so important to gather as much information as you can from other sources. For example, censuses can give ages, middle names and places of birth, all of which can narrow down the search. I always find it useful to scan my certificates, so that I have a copy in my online records as well as a hard copy.

Finally if you are looking for information regarding someone who was adopted, then check out:

www.adoptionsearchreunion.org.uk.

It wasn't until 1927 that the official registration of adoptions was introduced in England (1930 in Scotland and 1931 in Northern Ireland). Prior to this children were privately adopted and they may have never known. Some were adopted out by charities like Dr Barnardos and if you have an idea that this is the case, then it may be worth contacting the relevant organisation.

3 – Recording Your Research

After you have made that initial search over the last hundred or so years, your work may look something like this:

Mother – Jane Smith

Jane was born on the 14th July 1942 at 3 New Street, Brighton. She married William Thomas Jones on 4th May 1968 at Brighton Register Office.

At the time of her marriage she was living at 40 Shakespeare Road, Brighton. She was a Machine Operator.

Jane and William had 2 children; Geoffrey Stephen born on 22nd January 1970 and Jason John born on 17th July 1973. Both were born in Shoreham-by Sea, East Sussex.

Jane died of cancer on the 30th December 2004 in Brighton General Hospital.

Grandfather – John Smith

John was born on the 5th January 1904 at 15 Oakham Street, Brighton.

John married Anne Thomas on the 12th July 1928 in St Peter's Church, Brighton.

According to his marriage certificate John was a General Labourer.

On his daughter Jane's marriage certificate in 1968 it states he was a Factory Worker.

John died of chronic bronchitis on the 15th December 1978 at 17 Factory Road, Brighton.

Don't forget to reference all your sources!

One last thing I would like to mention here is the option to create a chart for your family tree, which is something that you may consider at this point in your research. Most of the major websites allow you to upload your ancestors' details into a tree.

These include Ancestry, Find my Past, genesreunited.co.uk and familysearch.org. You have a choice whether or not to make your tree public. Those who have public trees allow other subscribers to see them. This can be very useful when you reach a dead end, but BE VERY CAREFUL. As I have stated before, it is not wise to just take other people's records at face value. Use them as a starting point to further your own research when you hit a brick wall, but ALWAYS CHECK THE INFORMATION OUT FOR YOURSELF.

You may find that by messaging others that they will have proof that they can send you, but in my experience it is often the case that they have just taken the information from someone else and have no idea of the original source.

One plus side to all of this is that you may find relatives that you never knew about. Whilst tracing my own family tree I found 2nd and 3rd cousins from Australia, Canada and other parts of the U.K., some of whom I have kept in contact with.

There is a downside though, if you are not careful. When I started out I spent many, many hours just copying out information from other people's trees. In retrospect it was mainly a complete waste of time for reasons stated earlier. If you choose not to add your own family tree to one of these sites, you can still view other's trees and, if you are a subscriber, you can contact them for further details.

You can also build your chart by buying or downloading one of the various tree building software packages. I use Family Tree Maker, but there are others available.

Once you have traced the line back beyond 1911, then you can begin searching those all important censuses..

****

Chapter 3 – Censuses

1 – About the Censuses

The first British census took place in 1801 during the reign of George III. At first it was more or less just a population count, no individual's details being recorded.

In 1841, just after Queen Victoria came to the throne, the first more detailed census was taken. The facts that were recorded were their names, where they lived, their age (to within 5 years), their occupation, and whether or not they were born in the county that they then resided in.

From 1851 their exact age was recorded, also the town of their birth, their marital status, their relationship to the head of the house and whether they were blind, deaf or dumb.

Subsequent censuses have included various amendments.

In 1871 another category was added, whether idiot, imbecile or lunatic (all perfectly acceptable medical terms at the time).

From 1891 in Wales and 1901 on the Isle of Man, the language spoken was added.

In 1911 the length of marriage and the amount of children to the married couple (and how many still surviving) were also included. It also gives the number of rooms in the house, giving a clearer indicator to the size of the dwelling.

For the purpose of this chapter I will be mainly be referring to the censuses carried out in England and Wales. For Scotland and Ireland please see the relevant chapter.

These 10 yearly censuses have taken place ever since 1841 (apart from during the Second World War) and are available for the general public to view after 100 years.

Unfortunately, there will be an exception in 2031, as the 1931 censuses for England and Wales were destroyed in a fire in 1942 where they were kept in storage in Hayes, Middlesex. Ironically this was not caused by any enemy bombs and the exact cause of the fire has never been established. It was concluded that it was probably caused by one of the fire watchers carelessly discarding a cigarette end!

This might have meant that there was a huge gap in records between 1921 and 1951.

However, there are records of households in 1939 available, because in September of that year at the outbreak of war, the government carried out a survey in order to access who needed identity cards and later ration cards. This Register includes the names, addresses and occupations of the population of England

and Wales at the time, some 41 million people. These records are available to purchase on Find my Past. However, there is only unlimited access to them if you subscribe annually. They cannot be viewed as part of the monthly subscription package. In that case, they have to be purchased separately.

With regard to the 10 yearly censuses, schedules were handed out days before the allotted date to each household, and people were asked to complete the details of who was living in their house on the designated night. These details were then gathered by the enumerator who copied them into his book.

1911 is the only year where the original documents completed by the householders themselves still exist, so it is possible to see your ancestor's actual handwriting.

During the early years, only a small proportion of the population could read or write, so the enumerator would often have to take the information orally.

This accounts for a variety of errors including the variations of spelling of names that we often find in different censuses. Compulsory education did not come into England until 1870 (and even this was often waivered in agricultural areas).

In the earlier censuses you will find the symbols / and //. The former denotes the end of a household and the latter the end of a dwelling. This is a good indication of how cramped conditions might have been for your ancestors.

You will often see Do. written. This simply means ditto. The entry above is the same word as this one. Other abbreviations are also used. A useful website which gives a guide to these as well as other information about the censuses is census-helper.co.uk.

2 – Obtaining the Censuses

To view the censuses, you will need to subscribe to one of the websites that holds them online. (If you have the time and good access to your local library it is always worth checking with them because they often hold subscriptions to these websites and allow you to access them for free). Some County Archives also hold copies online or on microfilm and the National Archives at Kew also allows free viewing. However, subscribing yourself means that you have access 24/7 and can therefore research in your own time and at your own pace.

The websites that hold copies of all the original records are Ancestry and Find my Past. On these sites it is possible to see the entries for yourself. This is especially useful if the writing is slightly illegible as errors in transcripts can occur.

I would just note here that familysearch.org, which is a free website, does offer transcripts of the censuses, so this is also an option if you just want information. However, as I have stated before, please bear in mind the possibility of human error whilst transcribing the documents. I always look at original documents if they are available.

There is more than one way to look up the information you need. On Ancestry the best way is to click on the census you require on the home page (always work backwards from the latest one) then put the following in the search facility that comes up: name (you have a choice of an exact name or variants), age (always add at least a couple of years either way in the additional box as ages are not always recorded exactly) and place of birth (click on the correct place name that comes up in the drop box after you begin typing).

If it is a very common name (or you can't find it on the first search) then add additional facts such as the name of the spouse or parents. If you still have no luck then try omitting some of the search information, like where they were born. (County boundaries have changed over the years and sometimes this seems to confuse the situation).

On Ancestry there is another, although somewhat laborious way to find who you are looking for. I recommend this if all else fails. On the search button at the top, click on 'Census & Electoral Rolls' then where you have the option to 'Browse the Collections' complete the drop boxes until you get to the Civil Parish. It will then come up with a list of Enumeration Districts. If you are lucky there may be only 1 or 2 of these. If not you may have a long search on your hands. Click on each district and then go through each page of the census, carefully looking for names that might be your ancestor, but have been incorrectly transcribed.

On Find my Past the search is similar, but here you need to begin on the home page by putting in the name, year of birth (again with an option to search a few years either way) and place of birth. This will take you to all options available for that information. Click on the 'Census, Land and Surveys' option in the box. This will bring up a list of all the relevant records, starting with a list of the first available census and continuing chronologically. You will need to scroll down these, clicking through the pages until you get to the year you are interested in.

If you cannot find what you are looking for then go to the 'Edit Search' option and tick the boxes under the names to allow variations in spelling. If you still have no luck then remove the place of birth and perhaps add family members.

If after all this searching there is no trace of your ancestor, then move on. There are occasions, for whatever reason that people were missed off of the censuses. I have found this especially true in the 1841 records. The important thing is to find at least one census where the person whose name you know is a child, living with one or both parents. When you have this, you have a new name, a generation further back and the search can continue.

The one drawback to censuses is that because of reasons already explained, details in some of the censuses may not be totally accurate. As it was common for the information to be given by one member of the household, some facts might not be known. This is especially true if the person is a lodger or a visitor to the house rather than a family member. I am sure there were cases when any old information was given just to keep the enumerator happy.

Sometimes ages are inconsistent from one census to another. Perhaps an elderly relative is staying and their exact age has been forgotten, or perhaps a wife (or husband) has lied about their age to their spouse!

Places of birth are also variable. On one census a person might give the name of the actual hamlet they were born, in another a nearby town and perhaps in a third, just the county.

When these anomalies occur it is always worth looking at the general picture. If there is one inconsistency and everything else ties in, then chances are you have the right person. If you are still not sure, try looking at other censuses. If the Joe Bloggs you are uncertain of is in another year's census where you have already found your relative, then he is obviously not who you are looking for.

As you find each census, download it to your computer (or print it out if using a library or archive facility). As I have already mentioned, it is vital to keep all the information neatly in folders online and as hard copies. It's amazing how easy it is to end up with a complete jumble of information very quickly, so organisation is the key.

One last thing to mention here (and it is a trap I find myself falling into even now) is to assume that if you have found the person in some censuses, but then can't find them in subsequent ones, that this person has died. However, when you look for a death record, you can find no trace. If that person is a woman, then consider the fact she may have remarried. This was very common back in the days before the Welfare State. If a young woman was widowed with young children, finding someone to look after herself and her family would have been vital. It was often the case that widowed men would be the choice. She could look after his motherless children, he could bring home the bacon!

3 – What Do the Censuses Look Like?

See 2 examples overleaf.

Example of an 1891 census

Example of a 1911 census

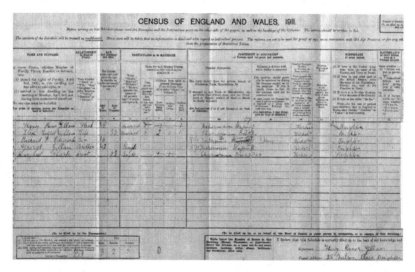

4 – Adding to Your Research

Once you have completed your search of all the available censuses, you can add to your original research like this:

Grandfather – <u>John Smith</u>

John was born on the 5th January 1904 at 15 Oakham Street, Brighton.

In 1911 he was living with his parents William and Mary and his siblings Eliza aged 17, Thomas aged 3 and Jane aged 3 months at 22 Albert Square, Brighton

John married Anne Thomas on the 12th July 1928 in St Peter's Church, Brighton.

According to his marriage certificate John was a General Labourer.

In 1939 John and Anne were living at 18 Tower Road, Brighton.[4]

John was still a General Labourer.

On his daughter Jane's marriage certificate in 1968 it states he was a Factory Worker.

John died of chronic bronchitis on the 15th December 1978 at 17 Factory Road, Brighton.

Great Grandfather – <u>William Smith</u>

William was born about 1872 in Brighton.

In 1911 William was living with his wife Mary and his children Eliza, John, Thomas and Jane at 22 Albert Square, Brighton. He was a Coal Man.

Chapter 4 - Birth, Marriage and Death - Part 2

1 – How Were These Events Recorded Before 1837?

Prior to 1538 very few records were kept. Before the dissolution of the monasteries in 1535, the monks were the principal record keepers. These records, for the most part, would have been limited to Royalty and the Gentry. So these elite, along with notable artists, writers, inventors and the like whose lives may have been documented by historians, were the exception. For the vast majority of people who were serfs and peasants, no written record would have been required or considered necessary.

However, in 1538 Thomas Cromwell, Henry VIII's chief minister, ordered that every wedding, baptism and burial was to be recorded. Every parson, vicar or curate of the parish was to make entries of every christening, wedding and burial. The parish had to provide a sure coffer with 2 locks, the parson having the custody of 1 key, the wardens the other. These entries were to be made each Sunday after service in the presence of one of the wardens. If these rules were not adhered to then a penalty of 3 shillings and four pence was issued, to be used for the upkeep of the church. (This penalty was later changed by Edward VI in 1547 to be put in the poor box).

There may be some gaps in parish registers between 1553 and 1558 when the Catholic Mary Tudor was on the throne.

Most of the early records were recorded on paper, often loose sheets, but in 1597 under the reign of Elizabeth I it was ordered that parchment books were to be used and the earlier records were to be transcribed onto parchment. Inevitably, some never were and have been lost. Also in 1597, a second copy of the records had to be made and sent to the Bishop annually.

There may also be gaps in the records during the English Civil War and Commonwealth (1642-1660), as records were poorly kept or hidden, and again some have been lost.

Various amendments were added over the following years, relating to penalties and what was to be entered in the registers. In 1812 it was ordered that baptisms, marriages and burials were to be entered in separate, specially printed books, 8 entries per page including more information.

Non-Conformists were those who 'did not conform' - in other words, did not belong to the Church of England. These groups might be Protestants (including Presbyterians, Baptists, Methodists, Independents, Congregationalists and Quakers) or Roman Catholics.

Most people prior to 1837 were baptised, married and buried in the local Church of England parish church, regardless of their beliefs. Even after the Toleration Act of 1689 granting the freedom to worship however one chose, many still registered these events in the local parish church. However, some Non-Conformist chapels and churches did keep their own registers.

For baptisms and burials these records continued to be the main source of record keeping until 1837. However, for marriages it was a different story. Prior to the mid 18th century, little attempt was made to control marriage. "Contract marriages" were common among the Protestant population. They believed that a marriage was binding without ceremony or rites so long as both parties agreed to the contract. This caused many problems as the agreement was unenforceable in law.

Clandestine marriages, or "Fleet" marriages, which were so called because they occurred mainly near the Fleet River in London (although they took place in other locales, as well), were marriages performed by a clergyman, but usually in secret with false licenses. In 1690 the government introduced a stamp tax on marriages in order to raise money and these clandestine marriages meant a serious lack of potential income from the tax. So in 1753, in an effort to regularise the solemnization of marriages, Hardwicke's Marriage Act was passed in England and Wales. It was effective from January 1754, and required that almost all couples had to be married in the Parish Church for the marriage to be deemed legal. Members of the Society of Friends (Quakers) and Jews were exempt from the Act and allowed to keep their own records.

The marriage was supposed to take place after banns had been called, in the home parish of one party, or else by licence. Banns are an official announcement of a marriage which is read out during the preceding weeks. This allows anyone who knows of a reason why the marriage shouldn't take place, to speak up. The marriage licence had to be obtained from the Bishop of the Diocese, or from one of his surrogates, and there was a fee to be paid. Non-Conformist couples often married by licence, as this could be obtained quickly and eliminated the need for banns to be called for 3 successive Sundays in a Parish Church they never normally attended.

From 1836 marriages were allowed to take place in Non Conformist places of worship providing they had been licensed to perform marriage ceremonies.

Mostly the churches only recorded the religious ceremonies, i.e. baptisms, marriages and burials, so it isn't always possible to find exact dates of birth and death. However, whilst we can be pretty sure that there is not much time difference between death and burial; birth and baptism is not so straightforward. Babies were usually baptised whilst still infants, but occasionally, for whatever reason, some were baptised much later. Often their age is recorded on the baptism records if they are not babies, but not always. Also, it is sometimes only the father's name on the baptism records, so without a relevant marriage record, the trail can sometimes end there.

The marriage records can often reveal interesting information such as whether or not a person was literate. A cross by a name and the word "mark" indicates that a person could not write. They can also tell us whether the individuals were widowed, and the man's occupation. Burial records also occasionally have interesting little snippets of information. E.g. William Brown – Ancient man!

2 – Obtaining Parish Records

Chances are that the first record you will want to look up is a baptism. The censuses will have given you a rough idea of when and where the person you are looking for was born. Bear in mind that if you only have them in the 1841 census that ages were rounded up or down so might be less accurate and it only stated whether the person was born in the same county as where they then resided. Also, as I have mentioned before, ages are also often inaccurate in other censuses, so don't be too rigid in your search. This is also true of places.

My first port of call is usually Ancestry or Find my Past. If you are not a subscriber, then familysearch.org and freesearch.org.uk do supply transcripts, but again I would emphasise how inaccurate transcripts can be.

If you are a subscriber to one of the websites then log in and input as much information as you have into the search facilities. You have options of doing a general search which will show any information that tallies with the name and dates you have put in, or you can be more precise and just click on the birth, marriage and death sections and then even more specifically, the births. This is my preferred method because if you start finding other information at this stage it is easy to get things jumbled up and confused. I always try (although not always successfully), to be as methodical as I can.

If you have no luck finding a match at this stage, try being a bit broader in your search. Instead of putting in a town, put the county; give a little more leeway in the dates and check the box that allows for variants in spelling. Remember names were often spelt differently in an age when not everyone could read. If an enumerator of the censuses was not familiar with the name, he might just write it down as he thought best based on the spoken word of an illiterate family member.

On the other hand, if you find there are just too many possibilities, then try being more specific. If you have the marriage certificate, you should have the father's name so add that to your search. If they lived with their parents in the censuses then you will have both names, even better.

As you narrow it down, it is worth checking each possibility. It is often the case that children were named after their parents or grandparents, so look for other family member names on the censuses. However, never take this fact alone as evidence as there were far fewer forenames used than there are now, and some names were very common. Occasionally if there is a very unusual name, then this might be a more precise indicator that you are on the right track.

If you still cannot find what you are looking for, then check on familysearch.org and freesearch.org.uk. Whilst these will only offer transcripts, they are better than no information at all, and may even lead to clues as to where you may find them on the other sites.

There are also other possibilities that might lead you to the information you seek. Useful sites that could possibly be of help are genesreunited.co.uk (this requires a subscription), parishregister.co.uk and one of the Online Parish Clerk websites (a list of these can be found at ukbm d.org.uk/online_parish_clerk). This list is not exhaustive and new websites are springing up all the time, so it might just be worth putting your ancestor's name in a search engine at this point, although unless it is a very unusual name, this is not very likely to help.

It may be that after all this you still have no luck and your online search might end there. At this stage it is worth looking into the possibility of finding a local family history group website or even visiting local archives. I will talk more about that later on in the chapter.

However, if you do find what you are looking for (which is most often the case) then you will find 1 of 2 things. Either there will be a transcript of the document or (if you are lucky) the original images will be available. If you subscribe to both aforementioned sites and one only has the transcript, then look on the other.

Different sites have different original document images and they are both adding to them all the time.

So you now have a baptism (and possibly a birth) date. This will show at least the father's name and probably both parents' names, (or just the mother's if the birth was illegitimate). If you already knew these from the censuses then it will confirm the research. If you didn't then it has added to the information and taken you back yet another generation.

Either way the next step is to find their marriage record. This is done in exactly the same way as finding the baptism (with different search options available). Likewise if you want to find burial records use the same route. There are also websites such as findagrave.com, billiongraves.com and deceasedonline.com that may be useful here. These are particularly helpful if you want to locate a grave. Having said that, the majority of people were buried in unmarked or simple graves that have long since gone to seed and are therefore not still locatable. It is useful to note here that prior to the Industrial Revolution (and in some cases for some considerable time after it), most people lived, married and died in the same small village or were married to someone in an adjoining village. This makes tracing them much easier than it would be today.

If you are lucky you may find that you can trace your ancestors back a long way, but unfortunately it is often the case that you meet a stumbling block or dead end along the way. If there is more than one possibility that the records you find belong to your ancestor, then don't guess. Best to just make a note of the possibilities and end there. Perhaps at some point, some clue will arise as to which record is correct and then you can move on safe in the knowledge that you are once again on the right track.

Once you have exhausted all genealogy website options then it is time to check out the local family history group sites. As I have stated before, it is always best to email or ring them first to see exactly what they can offer. Some (although few) will do a limited search for you for free, but most will charge a small subscription fee. Always check what you will get for your money. Sometimes they only offer services to people in person, but mostly they are broader in their approach and it is worth the fee. I have found that by joining some of these societies, I have been put in touch with other useful resources like local libraries and I even found people, who for a much smaller fee than the local archives charge, are willing to look up records on your behalf.

The final ports of call are the local archives themselves. If you are able to get to them then they are well worth a visit. Always check out what is available first. Make a list of everything you want to find (it's often best to wait until you have a few blanks in your tree to optimise your journey), then book an appointment. You will probably have to become a member which you should be able to do online, then you will need to take some ID with you, to confirm who you are. Local archives hold all available records, so if you draw a blank here then you can be pretty certain that unless somewhere out there someone owns a dusty old bible with the generations recorded in it, that you have come to the end of the road.

Accept it and move on to the next surname. That is a whole new journey!

3 – What Do Parish Records Look Like?

This varies a great deal but an example is shown below:

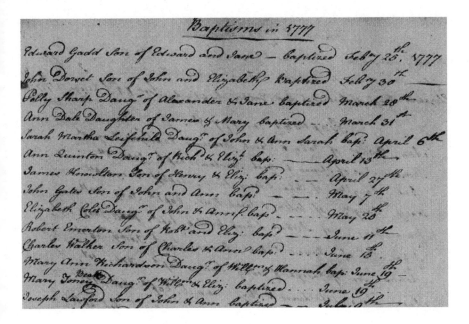

4 - Adding to Your Research

Let's update our hypothetical William Smith:

Great Grandfather – William Smith

William was born on 11th February 1871 at 17 Marine View, Brighton.

He was illegitimate.

In 1871 he was living with his grandmother Eliza, mother Margaret, Aunt Fanny and Uncle Benjamin at 19 Marine View, Brighton.

William married Mary Holmes on 12th July 1890 at Brighton Register Office.

At the time of his marriage he was living at 6 Claremont Row, Brighton and was a General Labourer.

In 1891 he was living with his wife and new baby James at 14 Newhaven Street, Brighton.

He was a General Labourer.

In 1901 he was living with his wife and children James and Eliza aged 7 at 60 Carlton Hill, Brighton.

He was a Coal Merchant.

In 1904 on his son John's birth certificate, William was living at 15 Oakham Street, Brighton.

In 1911 William was living with his wife Mary and his children Eliza, John, Thomas and Jane at 22 Albert Square, Brighton. He was a Coal Man.

William died on 25th September 1943 of carcinoma of the bladder at 31 Sussex Terrace, Brighton.

His daughter Eliza of 37 Sussex Terrace was present at his death.

Great x 2 Grandmother – Margaret Smith

Margaret was born in the first quarter of 1849 at 17 Crescent Cottages, Brighton.

In 1851 she was living with her parents and siblings at 28 Chapel Street, Brighton.

In 1861 she was living with her parents and siblings at 20 Marine View, Brighton.

In 1871 she was living with her mother Eliza, her son William, her sister Fanny and brother Benjamin at 19 Marine View, Brighton. (Between then and 1881, according to the next census, this property fell down!).

She was a Dressmaker.

There is no trace of Margaret on the 1881 census.

In 1891 she was living with George Mason as his housekeeper at 3 Claremont Row, Brighton.

In 1901 she was living with George Mason as his housekeeper at 20 Woburn Place, Brighton
.

Her occupation was given as Charwoman.

In 1911 she was living with her niece Ellen Johnson (her sister Fanny's daughter), Ellen's husband Henry, his brother George and Ellen's illegitimate son Richard at 28 Sycamore Place, Brighton.

Margaret never married.

She died on 9th May 1922 at 250, Elm Grove, Brighton (The Workhouse & Infirmary) of carcinoma uteri and cardiac failure.

At the time of her death she had been living with her sister Fanny at 37 Hardy Terrace, Brighton. She was listed as a Charwoman and Spinster.

Margaret was probably illiterate, at least at the time of William's birth, as only her 'mark' not her signature was on the birth certificate.

Great x 3 Grandfather - Jonathan known as John Smith

Jonathan was born on 3rd February 1810 in Chipping Barnet, Hertfordshire. He was baptised on 4th March 1810 in Chipping Barnet and again on 4th June 1812 at Jireh Chapel, Cliffe, Lewes.

Jonathan married Eliza Hurst on 26th March 1837 in St Andrews Church, Hove.

In 1841 he was living with wife and children James aged 3 and Fanny aged 1 in Essex Street, Brighton.

In 1851 he was living with his wife and children James, Fanny, Esther aged 9, Jonathan aged 7, Thomas aged 4 and Margaret aged 2 at 28 Chapel Street, Brighton.

His occupation was a Painter.

In 1861 he was living with his wife and children Esther, Thomas, Margaret and Benjamin aged 7 at 20 Marine View, Brighton.

He was still a Painter.

Jonathan died on 24th March 1866 at 18 Marine View,

48

Brighton, Sussex of cerebral effusion (brain haemorrhage).

Great x 4 Grandfather – <u>William Smith</u>

William was probably baptised on 14th August 1777 in Chipping Barnet, Hertfordshire.*

He married Esther Wilkins on 14th September 1807 at St Clement Danes, Westminster.

William was a widower when he married Esther.

In 1841 he was living with his wife at 17 St John's Street, New Shoreham.

He was a Railway Worker.

William died on 19th February 1847 at Nelson Place, Brighton of Old Age.

This is probably William because we know that his son Jonathan was baptised in Chipping Barnet. However, as we only have him in the 1841 census which gives no positive place of birth (other than it was not in Sussex), and as William Smith is such a common name, we can go no further at present.

By now you should be well on the way to having a good idea about at least one branch of your family tree. It's great knowing the names and abodes of your forefathers, but research becomes much more exciting when you begin to incorporate other factors. You may already have learned something from the censuses and birth, marriage and death records such as their occupations. Also you may have stumbled across some other information whilst doing those previous checks. Sometimes when you put a name into a search box on the websites, it leads you to other information about the person. When this happens I try not to let it distract me from the main name search, but I don't always succeed and find myself heading down another path, which can sidetrack me for a while.

My advice is, whenever possible, don't let yourself be distracted. Make a note of anything you think may prove to be useful and return to it later. Keep to the task in hand, it really does save confusion.

Whether or not you have come across other information, now is the time to begin thinking about it...

****

Chapter 5 – The Class System and Occupations

1 – Early Forms of Society in England

At the top of Celtic society was the king or chieftain. Below him were the craftsmen, then farmers. There was also a class of slaves. However, the Celts were a race of tribes and there was no political union amongst them, just a good deal of fighting.

When the Romans came to our shores, the higher members of society took on the Roman way of life, living in villas with luxuries such as windows and art. For the lower classes though life stayed much the same. They dwelt in simple huts and lived off the land. There were still slaves, who were simply the property of the rich.

When the Romans left, the standard of living took a backward turn.

At the pinnacle of Anglo Saxon society were the thanes who enjoyed hunting and feasting, but they lived in large crowded halls with no panes of glass and no chimneys. Below them were the churls who mainly rented land from the thanes. Some churls were rich, others were poor, but at the very bottom of society were the class of slaves known as thralls. For them life was very hard!

Until 1066 this primitive feudal system was evolving slowly with the emergence of small towns, but when William the Conqueror took over, he introduced a new system. The new king claimed all the land in England and divided it between himself (about 20%), the church (about 25%) and the remainder was given to Norman soldiers and nobles who had helped him conquer the country. All the land was still owned by the king, but the nobles or barons occupied and ruled over their own manor in exchange for providing services for him.

A manor consisted of a manor house, one or more villages, and land which consisted of meadows, pasture, woodland, and cultivated fields. The fields were divided into strips; one third for the lord of the manor, less for the church, and the remainder for the peasants. For the villagers at least half of the week was spent maintaining land belonging to the lord and the church. The rest of the time the villagers were free to work their own land.

WILLIAM the CONQUEROR.

The Feudal system was based on a social hierarchy. At the summit was the king, followed by the barons. The knights or vassals came next. They leased land from the barons and in return, they provided military service to the king at the time of need, and protected the baron and his family.

At the bottom of the chain were the peasants, also known as villeins or serfs. They were granted land by the knights, but they had to provide food and service to the higher classes on demand. They had no rights and they were also not allowed to marry without permission from their lords. They were not allowed to leave the manor.

During the 12th and 13th centuries with the expansion of trade, money rather than land ownership began to move society away from the feudal system. A new class of merchants trading in all sorts of goods sprang up, and serfs began to utilise this trade and pay for their farms with money rather than services. This led to the rise of the tenant farmer. By the end of the Middle Ages, many serfs had become able to purchase their freedom and most feudal lords had become landlords. Knights began to be replaced by large mercenary armies.

Despite the fact that feudal land tenure was not actually abolished in England until 1660, by the end of the 14th century many of the changes which were to result in the Renaissance in the following century, had taken place. However, the nobility did not disappear, they merely continued as an aristocracy.

The hierarchy now consisted of the aristocracy at the top, followed by the gentry (gentlemen who owned large amounts of land and usually had a coat of arms). Alongside them were the merchants who gained wealth in industries like wool processing, shipbuilding and banking. Below them were the yeomen who owned their own land and leased it to tenant farmers, also tradesmen who were crafts workers and shopkeepers. Tenant farmers or husbandmen followed and right at the bottom were the unskilled workers.

In the 16th century half of the population lived at a basic subsistence level which gave them enough food, shelter and clothes to survive. Humanist ideals were beginning to emerge, but the poor unskilled workers, particularly in rural areas in times of hardship, would still sometimes starve. In 1577 a church minister named William Harrison wrote in his work "A Description of England":

'We in England divide our people commonly into four sorts – gentlemen, citizens, yeomen, and labourers. First there are the gentlemen. After the king, the chief gentlemen are the prince, dukes, marquises, earls, viscounts and barons. These are called lords and noblemen. Next are knights, esquires and last of all those who are simply called gentlemen.' The latter probably included the merchants.

Harrison goes on to describe citizens as those who lived in cities and did important jobs. The yeomen, he declared, owned a certain amount of land and were 'well off'. Finally he described labourers and craftspeople as poor farm workers, tailors, shoemakers, carpenters, bricklayers and so on. He also added: 'As for slaves, we have none'.

However, despite the continuing hierarchy, for the first time, social mobility became possible. With hard work and luck, a farmer could become a yeoman. A yeoman could buy a coat of arms and become a gentleman. This could cost in excess of £100 (at a time when a decent house could be bought for £60), so it was by no means a possibility for all. Also a rich merchant might marry into the gentry or nobility. It was possible for an ambitious young man to rise in the world. But for the majority, the simple peasant labourers, their lot was unlikely to change. Their crucial, but humble role in society was, in part, reinforced by the Church. The belief was that God had created a 'Grand Chain' where every man played his part. Just as the king was there by Divine Right, so it was that those at the very bottom of society were there because it was God's will. To rebel against this could have consequences in the afterlife, so very few would have risked eternal damnation by attempting to change things. During the 18th century, the number of yeomen declined and the gap between the top and the bottom of society was larger. However, whilst their income and comforts may have been radically opposed, the 18th century artist William Hogarth saw similarities and depicted both ends of society as degenerate and corrupt. This is shown in the images 'Gin Lane' and 'Midnight Modern Conversation' below.

2 - Victorian Society

In Victorian society there were several layers to what had become known as the working classes. 3 out of 4 people did manual labour. The majority worked on the land, in domestic service and in factories as well as other manual trades such as building and mining. These labourers lived hand to mouth, so in times of sickness and as they grew older and less physically able, they might need to rely on charity or at worst would be forced to enter the workhouse. Right at the bottom of the social ladder was a form of underclass which consisted of petty criminals, prostitutes and chancers, commonly frequenters of gin houses; they were often homeless and destitute. However, most of the lower classes were hard working and on the right side of the law, and could for the most part, keep a roof over their head.

Within the family, when the children were very small, the wife would not be able to go out to work. She may do some work at home or take in lodgers, but usually the family would have been very poor. This meant as soon as the children were old enough they were sent out to work and the family's income would temporarily increase. The 1833 Factory Act stated that children under 9 were not allowed to work, those up to 13 could work no more than 9 hours a day and those up to 18 no more than 12 hours. They were also not allowed to work at night. This of course was not always enforced and young children were still employed in what we would consider arduous conditions in order for the families to survive.

However, eventually the children would leave and start their own families and the parents were left alone as they were becoming feebler and less able to work, so once again their standard of living would decrease.

The image below from Punch Magazine in 1856 shows crossing-sweepers. Children who would sweep aside horse manure so those of the more wealthy classes could cross the street without getting

THE CROSSING-SWEEPER NUISANCE.

dirty. Most people would probably have merely accepted this.

Social mobility, although becoming increasingly more possible, was still rare. Most people were born, worked and died in the same village or town with no prospect of improving their lot. Slightly above the unskilled and semi skilled labourers, although still considered working class, were the skilled craftsmen and artisans such as blacksmiths, tailors and millers.

The 1851 census showed there to be upwards of 1.5 million agricultural workers in Britain. By 1867 this number had dwindled to below 1 million and unskilled factory workers and domestic servants were ever increasing in numbers. Those who worked on the land were almost always the lowest paid with their average wage being about 14 shillings a week. However, they would have had an advantage over the town workers, who would not usually have had access to any land where they could grow or forage for food to subsidise their income. Factory workers may have earned as much as 22 shillings a week, whilst the aforementioned craftsmen could have expected to make on average 25 to 35 shillings.

After the working classes came the new breed of middle classes. They made up about 15% of the population. This group of people were diverse and included everyone from bankers, lawyers, doctors and the clergy as well as the lesser paid clerks (who might earn half the pay of a manual labourer) because income was not necessarily a factor. It was more a case of education. To be a clerk or a shopkeeper you didn't need a formal education, but you did need to be literate, something unnecessary for the lower class occupations.

Overleaf: A photo of a typical new middle class family.

The middle classes for the most part, consisted of hard working, church going individuals who resented the idleness of the aristocracy and looked down on the working classes who they considered to be less sober, pious and industrious than themselves. They valued education and aimed to send their children to private schools or one of the Grammar Schools that were now springing up.

Still right at the top was the elite class of land owning aristocrats and the gentry. Aristocrats (men who carried a hereditary title) could make up to £30,000 a year (compare that with an agricultural worker's £25 a year) from their land. They were expected to sit in Parliament and subsequently spent half their time in London.

The landed gentry, often known as Squires, were educated well bred men who spent most of their time on their estate taking an active interest in local issues. As the Industrial Revolution progressed and more and more people moved from the countryside to the town, the need for better working conditions increased. Trade Unions began to emerge and with the rights for the working man finally being recognised, the elite classes could no longer afford to exploit their labouring employees. The middle classes began to have more influence and with much more chance of upward mobility, the class system became more blurred. By the end of the 20th century there was still the basic Victorian 3 class system but the lower classes no longer lived on the breadline. The Welfare State and the NHS contributed to equality in health and social care. However a by-product of this Utopian ideal was the emergence of a new underclass. No longer the poverty stricken, but those who sometimes used the 'system' to their own advantage.

One last thing worth a mention here is the inequality between the genders. Until 1870, when a woman married, all her property became her husband's and despite getting the vote at the age of 30 in 1918, it was not until 1928 that the age was lowered to 21 to coincide with men.

3 – Obtaining Records that Give Clues to Your Ancestor's Occupation and Social Class

By now you will know many of your ancestors' occupations from the censuses and birth, marriage and death certificates. Occasionally you might be lucky enough to come across an occupation on older parish records if those who recorded them were more thorough in their work. However, there are other sources which may give you clues online.

On Ancestry in the Schools, Directories & Church Histories section you may find publications such as the Kelly's Directories which list the occupations of tradesmen, farmers, shopkeepers etc. Kelly's and other directories that can be found on Ancestry can be very useful because they can bridge the gap between censuses. Also, of course they are available for some time after the censuses.

On this subject, I was recently able to solve an ongoing family dispute for one of my clients. It was known that her great grandfather had been a publican for a while, but there was a difference of opinion between members of the family as to what pub he ran and in what village. From the 1901 census it was easy to conclude that one side of the argument was correct. However, I was also able to find an entry in Kelly's in 1899 which showed that at that time he was the landlord of the other pub in the other village, so it turned out that everyone was appeased!

Of course, these directories are not available yet for all counties, but new information is being uploaded all the time, so as I have mentioned before it is always good to retrace your research every now and then. Also, keep checking for what is new on the websites and opt to have emails sent when new information becomes available.

Like Ancestry, Find my Past has a wealth of useful directories, as well as transcripts of London Apprenticeship Abstracts from 1442-1850. As many young men were sent to London to be apprenticed at their trade, this can be a very useful resource for the early centuries.

Other records such as Wills, Probates and Tax Records are all possible useful sources that may give a person's occupation.

Last Wills and Testaments can be particularly useful. Of course they were only made by those who had money or property to leave behind, so they were certainly not drawn up for the majority. However, if you do have an ancestor who was a person of means, then they are sometimes a treasure trove of information. Many go back a long way and the wording can be quite hard to decipher (see below). With a little practice and patience though you should find that you can at least get the gist of what is written. More than anything, I have found that Wills confirm information already gleaned. As well as occupations, it may give the names of the spouse and children and place of residence etc. This can be a blessing if you are a little uncertain of some of your facts.

Both Ancestry and Find My Past have many original documents and transcripts of Will and Probate records of varying collections and again the National Archives website may be of help.

4 – How Did Your Ancestor's Occupation Fit into the Social Hierarchy?

There are far too many occupations and variables to list them all here, but there are several good websites which give an idea of what your ancestor's standard of living might have been like. This list is certainly not exhaustive, but it includes:

www.bl.uk/victorian-britain
www.bbc.co.uk/history/british/victorians
www.logicmgmt.com
www.census1891.com
www.worldthroughthelens.com
www.victorianweb.org

****

Chapter 6 – The Military

1 – The Royal Navy

The Royal Navy was officially formed in 1660 after the restoration of King Charles II. However, there had been a naval force, albeit in times of conflict in England, for at least a thousand years previous to that. By the end of the 17th century, the Navy had grown into a considerable force due to the continuing wars in Europe.

As the United Kingdom began to expand its Empire, the Royal Navy became the biggest maritime force in the world and indeed, is still the 2nd biggest force in NATO.

Up until the early years of the 19th century, particularly in times of war, a common method of obtaining men for the Navy was the press gang or impressment as it was known. This was perfectly legal. Able men, often from the Merchant Navy, but also ordinary labourers and apprentices were taken by force and made to serve their country.

2 – The British Army

It is often considered that the Restoration of 1660 also saw the birth of our modern British Army. However, 15 years prior to that, Oliver Cromwell had set up his New Model Army which was the first time that a full-time professional militia had been formed within the 3 kingdoms of England, Ireland and Scotland. They proved to be a considerable force, but after the Restoration they were disbanded, and on 26 January 1661, Charles II issued the Royal Warrant that created the first regiments of what was to become the British Army.

"The Battle of Waterloo" by Jan Willem Pieneman, 1824

The structure of this army has remained relatively unchanged to this day.

The Cavalry were troops who used horses, later replaced by tanks after the carnage of the First World War. The Artillery is trained to use heavy guns. The Engineers provide support for front line troops by carrying out and maintaining essential work such as bridge building. Finally and historically the most common was the Infantry – foot soldiers who are the front line attack in a conflict.

During the 18th century the public were wary of the amount of power government held if in control of a large army, so in times of peace the numbers were kept to a minimum. When extra men were needed they were raised by voluntary means or if that failed, by force. Several Recruiting Acts were passed which gave magistrates the right to press unemployed, but otherwise able-bodied men into service. These Acts also gave financial incentives to encourage enlistment. In 1757 this sum was £3, the equivalent of about 2 month's wages for a working class man.

3 – The Royal Air Force

The first powered airplane took to the skies on December 17th 1903 piloted by Orville Wright.

In 1912 the British government realised the potential of using aircraft in military situations and the Royal Flying Corps was formed as a part of the British Army. By the end of 1912 its aircraft consisted of 12 balloons and 36 aeroplanes. At the outbreak of the First World War in August 1914, the RFC went to France with just 63 aeroplanes. Its main task was aerial reconnaissance, but it soon became clear, that it could play a much larger role. By 1918 it had over 3000 aircraft in action.

In 1910 the Royal Navy acquired its first aircraft, and in 1914 the Royal Naval Air Service was formed. It was mainly used to defend the home territories. On the 1st April 1918 The Royal Air Force came into being by merging the Royal Flying Corps and the Royal Naval Air Service. By the end of the War on the 11th November 1918 just 7 months after its formation, the RAF had become the most powerful air force in the world with a total of 22,647 aircraft and 291,170 officers and men. All this in less than 15 years from when Orville Wright first took to the skies!

A First World War Recruitment Poster

The ranks of all 3 branches of the armed forces can be confusing and some ranks such as Warrant Officer and Corporal have been added over time.

Overleaf is a rough guide comparing equivalent ranks to help you ascertain how high up your ancestor was in the pecking order. In some cases, there may not be direct equivalents, but you should get an idea.

ARMY	ROYAL AIR FORCE	ROYAL NAVY
Field Marshall	Marshall of the Royal Air Force	Admiral of the Fleet
General	Air Chief Marshall	Admiral
Lieutenant General	Air Marshall	Vice Admiral
Major General	Air Vice-Marshall	Rear Admiral
Brigadier	Air Commodore	Commodore
Colonel	Group Captain	Captain
Lieutenant Colonel	Wing Commander	Commander
Major	Squadron Leader	Lieutenant Commander
Captain	Flight-Lieutenant	Lieutenant
Lieutenant	Flying Officer	-------
-------	-------	Sub Lieutenant
Second Lieutenant	Pilot Officer	-------
-------	-------	Midshipman
Warrant Officer Class 1	Warrant Officer	Warrant Officer
Warrant Officer Class 2	-------	-------
Staff Sergeant	Flight Sergeant/Chief Technician	Chief Petty Officer
Sergeant	Sergeant	Petty Officer
Corporal	Corporal	Leading Seaman
Lance Corporal	-------	-------
-------	Junior Technician/Senior Aircraftsman /Leading Aircraftsman	Able Seaman
Private	Aircraftsman	Ordinary Seaman

3 – Obtaining Military Records

Often, one of the first things that crops up, is "What did my father/grandfather/great grandfather do in the First World War?"

68

Unfortunately, over half of the service records from this time were destroyed during the Blitz, but many do remain.

If the person that you are searching for was killed during action, then the best place to visit online is the Commonwealth War Graves Commission (cwgc.org). The records here are free to search.

If however, they survived and you believe that they served in the British Army, then once again it is time to visit Ancestry and/or Find my Past. If you have been using these websites, then by now you should be familiar with the varying search facilities. Just use the drop boxes or sidebar searches to access what you are interested in.

These sites hold many of the surviving military records and are a good source, as they have images of the original hand written documents. They can tell you when the person joined up, where they were stationed, if they were hospitalised, whether they had good conduct, when they were discharged from the services and whether or not they were awarded any medals.

A good source for Royal Naval records, if you hold a subscription, is Find my Past. If not, then www.nationalarchives.gov.uk might be useful. These records will confirm date and place of birth and the sailor's rank and number. The search is free, but if you want further information, you can download the original images for a small fee. If you visit the National Archives at Kew you will be able to search the documents without charge.

Air Force records are to be found on Find my Past and www.nationalarchives.gov.uk

If you are content with just a short transcript to confirm that your relative was in the forces, then a visit to familysearch.org will probably be enough.

If all else fails and you happen to know the service number, then it might be worth checking forces-war-records.co.uk. As the transcripts only bring up a surname and an initial, without the service number it is not much help. This site is free to search, but if you find what you are looking for, then you will have to pay to view the transcript.

As well as the First World War, there are many other military records available on the previously mentioned websites. The censuses would have shown up any military personnel, so if this is the case then searching may well bring up the relevant documents relating to them. There are various records obtainable covering many conflicts, including the Crimean, Boer and even the Napoleonic Wars.

****

Chapter 7 – Crime in the 18th and 19th Centuries

1 – A Brief History of Crime in Victorian England

In the late 18th century and well into the 19th most of England only had unpaid Parish Constables to keep the peace in their town or village.

The first professional police force was founded in London in 1749 by Henry Fielding and initially consisted of 6 or 7 respectable men who were paid to prevent and detect crime. They carried truncheons, hand-cuffs and pistols and came to be known as the Bow Street Runners.

In 1798 the River Police were set up in London in order to deter the huge amount of criminal activity associated with the stealing of goods from merchant ships. This was a cleverly organised system operating between sailors and men on the shore.

The River Police also carried pistols!

The Metropolitan Police force was established in 1829 by Robert Peel.

These 'Bobbies' or 'Peelers' as they became known had, for the first time, a uniform and were paid 16 shillings a week. Initially they consisted of 1,000 men but steadily grew. The Bow Street Runners and River Police were incorporated into the new force and gained a uniform, but had to give up their pistols.

In 1851 the census identified 13,000 criminals in London. The proportion of criminals had probably not changed much over time, but with more crime detected and more access to newspapers; 'respectable' Londoners became more aware and more afraid of the lower classes.

Many boroughs and counties outside London began to employ their own police forces. They were still locally organised, because of the in built English resistance to the idea of a central force such as existed on the Continent, but in 1862 the government finally decreed that every town should have its own force.

The way in which criminals were perceived evolved over the 19th century. In the beginning there was an idea of the working class criminal at the bottom of society who was work-shy, drunken, lazy and immoral. By the middle of the century, this had formulated into the notion of a 'criminal class', those that dwelt in the slums and hovels of the inner cities. By the end of the century with the new vogue of psychiatry, much more emphasis was put on the idea that criminals had an abnormal behaviour pattern, brought about by either nuture or nature.

George Cruikshank's original drawing of the young pickpocket Artful Dodger with Oliver Twist looking on

This meant that the way in which criminals were treated changed over time. At the beginning of the century, it was still not uncommon for people to be hanged for what we today would consider petty crimes, (public hangings went on until 1868), but by the time Queen Victoria came to the throne, the only crimes punishable by death were murder and treason. By then transportation had became a common choice of punishment. This had been going on since the early 18th century when convicts were sent to North America. This of course, ceased when America gained her independence in 1776. From then on Australia was their destination. Between 1787 and 1868 an estimated 160,000 men women and children were sent half way around the world to serve their sentence. Most never returned as, although they were free to come back to England after their sentence ended, their passage was not paid, and so the cost would have been out of many's reach.

Ironically, many ex-convicts who stayed in Australia went on to prosper, and they and their families probably fared much better in the long run than if they had spent their time in a prison cell in England.

Prisons changed dramatically from the 18th century onwards. Initially they had developed into overcrowded 'dens of iniquity' where criminals were placed just to get them off the streets. They had easy access to alcohol and paid their gaolers, so the better off had a better deal. From the 1830s onwards new, larger prisons were built with the idea that prisoners should endure punishment. This punishment was generally pointless labour. One example was that inmates had to turn a crank 10,000 times during an 8 hour day. Officers could tighten the screws on the handles to make it harder – hence the slang term for prison officers – 'screws'.

By the 1860s prison reformers encouraged the idea that an attempt at reform was better than mere punishment and more constructive labour such as farming and mailbag sewing was introduced. This took a while to catch on everywhere, but by the end of Victoria's reign in 1901, catching and punishing criminals had undergone an overwhelming change for the better.

2 - Obtaining Criminal Records

To find out if anyone you are researching was ever charged with a criminal offence, the best source is (surprise, surprise!) Ancestry or Find my Past. Ancestry holds the England & Wales Criminal Registers from 1791 – 1892. These registers provide information about the charged individual, their trial and sentence (if convicted) or other outcome. Information listed may include: the name, age, birthplace, crime, when and where tried, sentence (death, transportation, imprisonment, acquittal, etc.), where and when received and date of execution or release.

Other records on this site include calendar of prisoners, court records, warrants, pardons and transportation records as well as UK Police Gazettes between 1812 and 1927 which contain printed publications used for communication between members of the police force.

Find my Past also offers images of many original documents for England & Wales from 1770-1935. These documents may give you a physical description (height, complexion, build, visage, eyes, hair), character description, marital status, offence, plea, sentence, name of magistrate or judge, previous convictions, petitions for pardons and more. Again local archives may also hold relevant records that are not yet available online. If you know that your ancestor committed a crime and the date on which he was tried, it is well worth searching through the old newspapers which most archives hold.

Often using all of the available resources can complete the picture. I found the story of my ancestor (the wonderfully named Cephas Tree previously mentioned in Chapter 1) and his run-in with the law. Using the 2 websites and then travelling to the

Keep (the East Sussex archive), I was able to get original images of his burglary conviction for which he was sentenced to hang along with his daughter Mary! I then found images of the reduction in their sentences to transportation, then Cephas' final pardon. At the archives I found some wonderful newspaper reports. According to the Brighton Herald 21st March 1807, when the guilty verdict and death sentence was announced "Mary Tree, pierced with horror, convulsed and screaming, was borne from the court". Mary was transported to New South Wales on the Speke which set off in March 1808. She settled there and hopefully lived happily ever after. Cephas spent the rest of his life in his home town of Brighton and died in 1816 at the age of 70.

Below is an example of a Criminal Register which includes another of my relatives, Esther Orchard who was convicted of larceny in 1845! I don't think I come from a particularly 'criminal class'. When all considered, for those hailing from the working classes in Victorian Britain with all its poverty, it is not surprising that the temptation to steal was often too strong to resist.

Chapter 8 – The Poor Laws and the Workhouse

It is quite likely whilst you are doing your research that you will come across someone who, for one reason or another, had a stint in the workhouse.

The word 'workhouse' implies that the sole purpose of the institution was to give people employment. However, the workhouse was more than that. It provided an infirmary for those that couldn't work and often acted as a temporary refuge for those in need.

An example of this was my own grandfather who was born in the Brighton workhouse in 1888. He was illegitimate and it is likely, either that his mother was rejected by her family or that there was some kind of medical problem that required more than a midwife.

His mother, my great-grandmother was also illegitimate and her mother never married nor had any more children. It fell upon her to bring up my grandfather (her grandson) whilst his mother got married (presumably not to his father) and went on to have 8 more children. She lived just a few streets away.

The stigma of illegitimacy was such that it was rare for men to take on a child that was not their own, born out of wedlock. Perhaps that is why my great-great-grandmother never married. I like to think that her love for her daughter was more important than her need for a man. Of course this is probably just wishful thinking, something that you will find yourself doing a lot during your research!

1 – Early Poor Laws

Before the 14th century giving help to the poor was based on a purely voluntary, charitable basis. However, as is often the case with human nature, this could be taken advantage of. Able-bodied men could and would become beggars.

After the Black Death in 1349 there was a shortage of labour which forced up wages and meant some land went unused. The consensus amongst the landowners was that all able-bodied men should work. This led to the Statute of Labourers in 1351 which stated that all men who were able had to work and it made it illegal for anyone to give aid to able-bodied beggars.

In 1388 the Statute of Cambridge was passed that made each Hundred (an old administrative unit within a county) responsible for its own labourers and the infirmed.

These Acts were followed over the next 2 centuries by many others. The Vagabonds and Beggars Act of 1495 stated that:

"Vagabonds, idle and suspected persons shall be set in the stocks for three days and three nights and have none other sustenance but bread and water and then shall be put out of Town. Every beggar suitable to work shall resort to the Hundred where he last dwelled, is best known, or was born and there remain upon the pain aforesaid."

The 1531 Vagabonds Act allowed for designated areas to beg, but this was usually limited to the infirmed. Any begging outside of these areas incurred harsh penalties.

In 1547 the Statute of Legal Settlement stated that an able-bodied beggar could be enslaved. However, it also decreed that houses should be built for the impotent poor, those too sick or elderly to work, and that they should be relieved or cured.

In 1572 after a trial run in several cities, the poor rate was introduced and administered by overseers who determined how the money was spent and to whom it was given.

In 1597 the Act for the Relief of the Poor was passed requiring all parishes to appoint an overseer who was responsible for finding work for those capable and looking after those who weren't.

It is interesting that the money raised by the poor rates was based (as is still the case with Council Tax) on the value of someone's property. As now this was not the responsibility of the owner of the property, but the tenant. Hefty fines and even prison could result in failure to pay these rates. How little some things change!

The next big amendment was the Settlement Act of 1662. The rules for 'settlement' had their roots in the long established laws of the 14th century. A man or unmarried woman's place of settlement was that of their father. If a child was illegitimate then it was the place of their birth. This led to many unmarried pregnant women being taken to another parish just before the child was born. A married woman's place of settlement was that of her husband.

If work was scarce and a man wanted to seek work outside of his parish, he required a document which stated that should he not be able to support himself and his family in his new place of residence, then they were entitled to send him back to his place of settlement.

In 1697 an Act was passed requiring those who begged to wear a "badge" of red or blue cloth on the right shoulder with an embroidered letter "P" and the initial of their parish. This was rarely enforced and didn't last long. Later Acts allowed for other ways to obtain settlement. Apprentices (some as young as 7), could claim their place of apprenticeship. Labourers who had worked continually for a year in one place could also claim settlement. Often contracts were given for 364 days and sometimes labourers who were not happy in their new place of work would make sure they moved on before the year was up. These settlement laws were amended many times in the subsequent centuries and were not finally abolished until 1948!

Overleaf is a copy of my great x 3 grandfather's settlement certificate. He was a ropemaker and set off to Hastings to find work. His son Cephas (you may remember him from chapter 7) was the one set to commit burglary in his later life.

2 – The New Poor Laws and the Workhouse

The idea of the workhouse had been around since at least the 14th century, but in the 17th century it became more popular. The poor were a financial burden on the parish and by denying 'out-relief' to the able-bodied and forcing them to work in order to survive, they could save money. In 1723 the Workhouse Test Act gave parishes the option to make the workhouse the only choice for those who were capable of work. By the 1770s there were around 2,000 such workhouses in the country, housing nearly 100,000 people. Inmates were set menial tasks such as spinning or sewing and had to adhere to strict rules. A few workhouses were run well. They were clean and offered basic education and health care. Other workhouses, however, were overcrowded and full of disease. In the 1750s social investigator Jonas Hanway discovered that the death rate amongst workhouse children in London was over 90%. This meant some of the poor were prepared to starve rather than enter their walls.

The Relief of the Poor Act of 1782 enabled parishes to form unions known as Gilbert Unions to build and maintain larger workhouses to accommodate the infirmed and elderly. They were to find able-bodied workers employment with land-owners, farmers and other employers who received allowances from the poor rates, and to give the labourers relief until work was found. However, not many of these unions were formed and by the 1830s most parishes had at least one workhouse.

The Poor Law Amendment Act of 1834 aimed to end all out-relief for the able-bodied. Poor Law Unions were formed from the 15,000 or so parishes in England and Wales and each union had its central workhouse. This led to a further 500 workhouses being built over the following few years. Ireland and Scotland were to set up similar schemes in the following decade.

George Cruikshank's original drawing of the young Oliver Twist asking for more

Despite this Act many parishes still preferred to offer out-relief to those with sickness in the family, as it was more cost effective than boarding them in the workhouses. The 1844 Outdoor Relief Prohibitory Order reinforced the idea that all out-relief to the able-bodied poor be abolished.

However, in 1846, of 1.33 million paupers, only 199,000 were maintained in workhouses, of whom 82,000 were considered to be able-bodied, leaving an estimated 375,000 of the able-bodied on out-relief.

The workhouse was not intended to be a pleasant place. Men, women, children, the infirm, and the able-bodied were kept separate and were fed basic rations of gruel, bread and cheese. They were forced to wear rough uniforms and were only allowed to bath under supervision once a week. Many of the able-bodied were given arduous or monotonous work such as stone-breaking or removing the hemp from telegraph wires. Another favourite was picking apart old rope know as oakum. Parents were allowed very little contact with their children, perhaps an hour or so a week on a Sunday.

In 1848 The Times suggested that 90% of 14 year old girls who left the workhouse ended up working as prostitutes. Although the law surrounding the age of consent is rather complicated at that time, in England the age was just 10! This was raised to 12 in 1861 and to 13 in 1875, but it was not until 1885 that the Criminal Law Amendment raised the age of consent to 16.

Gradually, through various Acts and through outrage of the more caring members of society, things began to improve in the workhouses.

The basic rations began to include more wholesome food and occasional treats and outings were allowed.

The Diseases Prevention Act of 1883 allowed for treatment of all in the workhouse infirmaries, not just the poor, and some began to operate as private hospitals. By the end of the century about 30% of the population aged over 70 was in workhouses. This led in part to the introduction of the old age pension.

From 1913 onwards, the term "workhouse" was replaced by "Poor Law Institution", and in 1929 this changed again to "Public Assistance Institution". Officially, the workhouse was abolished on the 1st April 1930, but the buildings continued to be used to house the elderly, chronically sick, unmarried mothers and the homeless. Even after the National Health Service was formed in 1948, the former workhouse buildings continued to be utilised for the care of the elderly and chronically sick.

Gradually since then, some of the old workhouse buildings have been demolished or fallen into decay, but many still exist as part of new hospitals, care homes, residential homes or business premises.

If you are interested in finding out more about the Poor Laws and workhouses then www.workhouses.org.uk is an extremely informative website which includes detailed information about the various workhouses throughout the country.

3 – Obtaining Poor Law and Workhouse Records

You may find that your ancestor spent time in the workhouse from one of the censuses or a birth certificate, but bearing in mind these are only a snapshot into their lives, it is possible that they did have a stint in the workhouse in between these years.

Find my Past has a selection of valuable records from several counties including the London Poor Law Records from 1581 – 1899. Ancestry also holds a small selection of county records as well as London, England, Workhouse Admission and Discharge Records from 1659-1930, London, England, Poor Law and Board of Guardian Records from 1430-1930 and London, England, Selected Poor Law Removal and Settlement Records from 1828-1930.

In this instance however, the best source of information is likely to be the local county archives. They will hold workhouse records as well as settlement certificates and other records that may indicate that your ancestor was affected by the Poor Laws. The National Archives website, discovery.nationalarchives.gov.uk will be useful here and the workhouses.org.uk website gives a list of all the archives of interest.

When most of us start to delve into our family history we are often hoping to find somebody rich or famous. The sad, but often more interesting truth is, we are far more likely to be descended from someone who experienced poverty, hunger and severe hardship during their life time!

****

Chapter 9 – Death and Disease

In Britain in the 21st century if a member of our family dies, particularly if that person is not considered old, it is felt as a time of great loss and waste of a life. It is easy to think that it would have been easier for our ancestors because they experienced far more loss of life at an early age than we do now. However, as humans we are programmed to care for and look after our family and this is a trait that has evolved in primates for millions of years. It makes no sense to believe that the loss we feel was not equal to the loss felt by our ancestors, however common the situation was.

1 – The Middle Ages

Almost nothing was known about the causes of disease at this time. Most doctors believed as the Greeks had done, that illness was caused when the 'Four Humours' i.e. phlegm, black bile, yellow bile and blood became unbalanced. Demons, witches, the stars and bad smells were just a few of the reasons that the medieval population believed to be responsible.

There was some form of progress during this time though. Doctors developed the first painkillers in the form of opium, and wine was used as an antiseptic. It is now believed that medieval towns would have been cleaner than those of later times. Towns were less crowded and some even had public bath houses. Parliament passed the first law requiring people to keep the streets and rivers clean in 1388. However, none of these precautions could stop the spread of the most infectious and deadly diseases.

The Black Death or Plague swept across Europe between 1346 and 1353. It reached the shores of the British Isles in June 1348 via Dorset. 2 months later it devastated Bristol, England's second largest city and major port. It hit London in September and spread its way across England into Wales, Ireland and eventually Scotland in 1350.

The Black Death was an epidemic of bubonic plague, a disease caused by the bacterium yersinia, spread by fleas. It is found in wild rats, usually black rats. It can take up to 2 weeks for the disease to destroy the entire population of the rat colony and for another 3 days the fleas lie dormant until the threat of starvation forces them to feed on humans. The bites cause buboes, swellings in the lymph nodes, hence the name bubonic plague. In the cities, victims were thrown into large mass graves, as many as 200 a day were 'disposed' of in this way.

With the rise of urban populations and the expansion of trade with Europe during the Middle Ages, the disease was able to spread quickly. Most people believed it to be the will of God who was punishing them for their sins.

In 1349 Edward III ordered that the polluted and overcrowded city of London be cleaned up, but all the street cleaners had died of the disease!

The Black Death was not prejudiced in its victims. It affected both rich and poor, killing Archbishops as well as peasants. It is thought to have killed between a third and a half of the population, some rural villages losing as much as 80 to 90% of their inhabitants.

By 1350 the Black Death had run its course in Britain, but it returned sporadically (although less destructively) until the late 17th century. Later outbreaks were particularly fatal for children and young people. It's sad to think of all the parents who must have wept for the loss of their little ones.

During the Middle Ages if you survived the Black Death it was no guarantee that you would survive into old age. There were many other dangers that could prove fatal.

In the early 14th century there was 'The Great Famine'. From 1300 Europe experienced a 'Little Ice Age' and between 1315 and 1322 there was incredibly heavy and prolonged rainfall. Farmers struggled to produce crops and between 10 and 15% of the English population died of starvation.

It is estimated that between 20 and 30% of children (and quite possibly a lot more) died under the age of 7 during the medieval period. Diseases such as measles, whooping cough, smallpox and tuberculosis were just a few of the many that were the cause of such a great loss of young life.

Malnutrition and infections were common and a mother who was undernourished would not have provided sufficient immunity in her breast milk to sustain her infant.

Even in wealthy families it is estimated from records that between 1330 and 1479 one third of the all children of Dukes died before the age of 5. Childbirth itself was fraught with danger. Breech births, haemorrhaging and simple exhaustion could prove fatal and post natal infection was also common. Life itself was hazardous during these times. Simply travelling from one place to another could cause death from exposure or violence. Accidents from those caused by hunting, to the lack of safety in the home, were common.

Hospitals have been around since the Middle Ages. In 1247 the Priory of St Mary of Bethlehem was founded in Bishopsgate by Simon Fitzmary, the Sheriff of London. It was originally developed as a place of healing for sick paupers, but by the turn of the 15th century it was largely dedicated to the treatment of the 'insane'. This not only included those with mental health problems, but also those with learning difficulties, dementia and epilepsy. The regime consisted of punishment and religious worship, both of which were considered to be useful tools in aiding recovery. This institution came to be known as Bedlam.

"Bedlam' from William Hogarth's 'A Rake's Progress' c. 1733

However, the vast majority of those both mentally and physically ill would not have been institutionalised. Their treatment would have included an array of 'cures'. Some like the application of leeches is now realised to have some benefit, whilst others such as whipping to earn God's forgiveness were clearly steeped in superstition and were of no benefit to the patient.

2 – The 16th to 18th Centuries

During this era people were still unaware about germs and how diseases were spread. Filthy water and faeces would be thrown into the streets and personal hygiene such as hand washing was not deemed to be necessary.

The Plague was still affecting England during the 16th century. Of those affected at this time about half died. Over a quarter of London's population was wiped out.

Between 1643 and 1652 the Civil War raged across England. The conflict left some 34,000 Parliamentarians and 50,000 Royalists dead, while at least 100,000 men and women died from war-related diseases, bringing the total death toll in England to almost 200,000, about 4% of the population at that time. More died in Scotland, and far more in Ireland.

In 1665 another great outbreak of Plague occurred. It began in London in the poor, overcrowded parish of St. Giles-in-the-Field. By June more than 6,000 people had died and just 2 months later the toll had risen to more than 30,000. This was 15% of London's population at the time. By the end of the year the disease was almost eradicated and the Great Fire of London the following year which destroyed much of the filth ridden city was a blessing in disguise as London was cleansed.

Before antibiotics, bacterial diseases such as syphilis and cholera could often prove fatal. Cholera was caused by drinking contaminated water. Before the installation of proper sewerage systems outbreaks were commonplace.

Another huge killer was Typhus. In the filthy crowded conditions of the cities and the lack of hygiene of the majority, body lice were common. If a person scratched and the faeces of the lice entered the bloodstream then it was often a swift and painful death. Many criminals, some in jail for petty crimes, died in the squalid conditions of the city prisons.

Smallpox was also common. Queen Elizabeth herself contracted it in 1562 when she was 29 years old. Although she survived, it left her bald and she had to cover the scars on her face with thick white make up (made from white lead and egg whites!) for the rest of her life. Dysentery, scarlet fever, influenza, pneumonia and all the other aforementioned diseases were still common causes of death in children.

'The King's Evil' was the name given to scrofula, the swelling of the bones and lymphatic glands in the neck caused by tuberculosis. In England and France from the time of Edward the Confessor it was believed that the disease could be cured by a royal touch.

Subsequently, monarchs would hold ceremonies where hundreds of people suffering from the disease would kneel before them and touch their hand.

James I thought it mere superstition but after the return of the monarchy following the Commonwealth period, Charles II restarted the ceremony. The ceremony concluded with a reading from the Bible, prayers and a blessing. Then the monarch's hands were washed.

In 1712 Queen Anne touched Samuel Johnson who was then a 2 year old boy. The practice ended with Anne, the final Stuart monarch, but continued in France until 1825.

Perhaps more surprising than the aforementioned diseases, malaria was the cause of many deaths around the Thames during this period. The swampy theatre district of Southwark was particularly at risk.

Accidents were still common. Drowning in wells and bathtubs was the most reported accidental death in children under the age of 5.

3 – The Industrial Revolution

Towards the end of the 18th century the Industrial Revolution was beginning to take hold in Britain. Villages and small cottage industries were being rapidly replaced by towns, cities and factories. It was a time when there was little or no regard for the workers' health or safety, and danger was everywhere.

Workers had to endure long hours of labour, machinery was often exposed and conditions were hot and crowded. Exhaustion could lead to a lack of concentration which in turn led to a higher risk of injury. Children were employed to clean up, moving between the machines. The long hours meant that during the winter months, workers would see no daylight. As well as the many accidents amongst the children, rickets due to lack of vitamin D obtained mainly from sunlight, was common.

Until 1842 children as young as 5 could be 'bought' to work down the mines Because of the cramped and unhealthy conditions they could develop distorted bodies and lung disease as well as risking death from the causes mentioned below.

Likewise, until as late as 1875, young children could be used as chimney sweeps. This could not only cause the obvious problems of such an occupation, but also a disease that my own great x 2 and great x 3 grandfathers died from at a relatively young age – chimney sweep's cancer. This was a form of cancer that affected the scrotum, and was caused by the friction of filthy, sweaty clothes when sweeps were sifting soot. The cancer began as a superficial sore with hard, rising edges that worsened over time. The only known cure was the removal of the infected organ. Few sweeps (including my ancestors), with their general mistrust of all forms of institution were willing to put themselves through such an ordeal.

Meanwhile the ever increasing number of factories required more and more power, and the coal mining industry expanded to accommodate this. The dangers for overworked, underpaid miners were just as hazardous as those working in factories. Many were killed by gas, explosions, or due to tunnels caving in.

During the 19th century well meaning reformers brought about change. Various Factory Acts between 1819 and 1847 limited the hours worked by children and women. By 1874 no factory workers were allowed to work more than 56½ hours per week.

Despite the horrors of industrial labour, millions flooded into the towns and cities seeking work. This kept wages low and exploitation by the middle class factory owners was the norm.

The influx of so many people caused even more overcrowding and poor sanitation.

Industrial Britain was hit by several outbreaks of cholera in the years 1831-32, 1848-49, 1854 and 1867. In the early 19th century the Thames was an open sewer system and was also used as a source of drinking water. It was not until Dr John Snow proved that disease was spread by bacteria rather than smell, and 'the Great Stink' in the summer of 1858, that plans for a proper sewerage system that diverted waste to the Thames estuary were drawn up by Joseph Bazalgette. The sewers were completed around 1870 and are still in use today.

Smallpox was still around despite Edward Jenner's vaccine of 1798. Many people were either unaware or wary of it.

Typhoid, another water born disease and typhus were still very prominent, particularly in the cities.

Tuberculosis is a highly contagious disease caused by inhaling droplets of sputum from an infected person. It was the highest cause of death in the cities and it is estimated that it was responsible for a third of all deaths between 1800 and 1850. However, by the end of the 19th century with the discovery of the need for better sanitation and hygiene and with the rise of the Trade Unions, the causes and number of deaths was on the decline.

4 - 20th Century

During the late 19th and early 20th centuries more vaccines were discovered for diseases such as diphtheria, tetanus, whooping cough and tuberculosis, followed in the 1950s by the Polio vaccine. By 1980 it was announced that smallpox, such a common and virulent disease in the past had been eradicated worldwide.

Better working conditions meant a safer working environment and an increase in wages meant better nutrition for the working classes.

By far the biggest concentrated loss of life during the 20th century was caused by war.

The figures relating to British casualties of the First World War are very hazy. Estimates vary according to different sources. Between 700,000 and 1 million soldiers lost their lives whilst an estimated 2 million were wounded. Civilian losses are estimated to be about 31,000.

But as the war ended and peace was on the horizon, the worst global pandemic in history struck – the Spanish Flu. It is estimated to have killed over a quarter of a million Britons alone, but by mid 1919 the disease disappeared as quickly and unexpectedly as it had arrived.

Estimates for the Second World War also differ. Somewhere between 300,000 and 400,000 military personnel died and between 60,000 and 70,000 civilians. The contrast between the 2 wars is noticeable. Roughly half as many soldiers died, but twice as many civilians. This is a devastating number, but only represents about 1% of the British population, fewer than the estimated 2% of the population who died in the First World War and even fewer than those who lost their lives 300 years earlier during the English Civil War.

During the 20th century and up to today the causes of death and disease have dramatically changed. Infant mortality rates at the beginning of the century were nearly 30 times higher than they are now. With the continuing worldwide research into health, people are living much longer. In 1901 only 20% of the population lived beyond 65, today it is around 80%. This has meant a shift in the causes of death. Due to the discovery of antibiotics and further vaccination programmes, many infectious diseases have been all but eradicated. Our better understanding of hygiene means the likes of cholera, typhus and typhoid are diseases of the past. Today the leading causes of death are heart failure, dementia and cancer.

5 – Obtaining Information About the Diseases and Deaths of Your Ancestors

It is easy to discover what your ancestors died of if they passed away after the introduction of death certificates. However, sometimes the cause may be something unfamiliar to us. There are several websites that give lists of old names for modern diseases, but it is probably best to just google it. Some of these illnesses are a product of their time.

Finding instances of disease and death prior to the introduction of registration is really pot luck. Most parish records just give burial dates with no mention of a cause of death. Occasionally, particularly in cases of infectious diseases such as smallpox, the cause may be recorded. I have found this written in the margins on several occasions.

Sometimes there might be obvious clues. If a mother dies shortly after the birth of a child, it might be safe to assume there were complications or an infection involved. Of course there is no certainty. If several members of a family die close together at the time of an epidemic, again this could be an indicator. Most illnesses and accidents that do not result in loss of life are rarely going to be recorded, but occasionally you might get lucky. 2 examples are shown below.

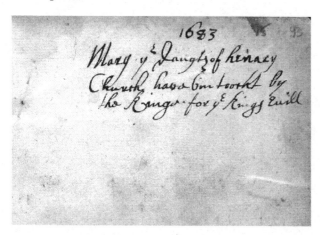

A record of a child who had been 'touched' by the King – Mary survived, perhaps the King did have a 'magic' touch!

As George Ruddell, aged 9 years, living in East-street, was crossing the Old Kent-road on Saturday, he was knocked down and run over by a horse and cart, and sustained a fracture of the thigh.

Taken from the London Press, December 21st 1867

The best source of newspaper records, if you have a subscription, is Find My Past.

You can also use www.britishnewspaperarchive.co.uk which has a wide source of information. The records are available by paid subscription or pay as you go credits. If you can get to local libraries or archives you have an even better chance of finding a juicy titbit about an ancestor. However, these records are often not indexed or digitised, so unless you are aware of the date a particular event, it can very laborious, working your way through pages of microfilm. There are other websites that concentrate on particular newspapers and areas, and a good source of information on these is in the newspaper research guide at www.nationalarchives.gov.uk.

You might be lucky enough to find the last resting place of an ancestor. Of course you can wander around churchyards if you know the parish in which they were buried.

Also, as mentioned before, websites that might be of use are:

www.deceasedonline.com
www.findagrave.com
www.billiongraves.com

However, bearing in mind that most people were buried without headstones and that the stones break and disappear over time, it is unusual to find very old graves.

There is one last thing to mention with regard to burial records and headstones. Don't take the age given too literally and end up basing other research on it. These ages are not set in stone (not metaphorically anyway - if you pardon the pun).

As with the censuses, particularly in older people, ages might have been forgotten, or those left behind simply may not know. In a time before old age pension, the only age that really mattered was 21, when you became an adult and were able to leave an apprenticeship or get married without parental consent. After that, age became pretty much irrelevant. It was just a number!

****

Chapter 10 - Education and Apprenticeships

1 – The History of Education in Britain

Formal education was first seen in Britain at the time of the Roman Occupation, but as with most of the advancements that the Romans brought, this almost certainly disappeared when they left.

The first known school was established in Canterbury in 598 by St Augustine who needed an establishment to teach priests Latin.

'Grammar schools' as they were then known gradually expanded their curricula to include mathematics and science.

During the Viking invasions which began at the end of the 8th century, education once more fell into decline, but after the Norman conquest of 1066, it flourished and began to become more secular. By the end of the 13th century Universities began to develop.

During this time more 'independent schools' became established. The word independent meant independent from the church, not from the state as it has come to mean today. These brought education to the children of the 'upper classes', but also began to include charitable organisations for poorer children.

Although it is not possible to be completely accurate, it is estimated that in the 16th century only 20% of adult males could sign their name and only 5% of women.

Of course this varied enormously between the classes. Aristocrats, gentry and rich merchants were almost totally literate by 1600, but most labourers could not read at all.

In Elizabethan times the Renaissance brought new ideas about philosophy and art, and some schools began to incorporate these into their teachings.

By the end of the 17th century it is estimated that the amount of those who could sign their name had risen to 50% of men and 25% of women.

By the beginning of the 18th century the curriculum in schools was beginning to take on its modern form and included mathematics, geography, modern languages and science.

However, schooling was far from within the reach of everyone. There were parish schools funded by charities and wealthy patrons, but they were not in every village and with the growth of urbanisation most children from poorer families received no education at all. If a child went to school, he could not earn any money for the family, and his income could often mean the difference between eating and starvation.

Girls in particular were unlikely to receive any schooling. Even in wealthier families girls were mostly taught at home by governesses and their education would often have included less academia and more practical work such as sewing or spinning. In the 1780s the Sunday School movement began. This meant that boys who worked all week could at least have some form of education. These schools were initially designed for the poorer 'workhouse' children to teach them not only to read and write but to instil Christianity into them.

In the 1830s Parliament began to get involved and money was put aside to build free schools for poorer children.

"February – Cutting Weather – Squally" by George Cruikshank 1839

At the beginning of the Victorian age it is estimated that more than 1 in 3 Englishmen were illiterate and half of all women.

In the 1840s the 'Ragged Schools' were becoming popular. These were charitable schools for destitute children and catered mainly for the urban poor of the industrial cities. The Ragged School Union was established and some resources for free clothing and even lodging were provided. By 1870, at their peak, there were 250 of these schools in London and 100 outside the capital.

THE RAGGED SCHOOL.
In West Street (late Chick Lane) Smithfield
Drawn by George Cruikshank about 1843-4.

In 1857 the Industrial Schools Act was intended to solve problems of juvenile delinquency, by lawfully removing poor and neglected children from their home environment to a boarding school. In 1870 a new Act was passed that began to make provision for all children to have elementary education. In 1880 it was made compulsory for all children aged between the ages of 5 and 10 to attend school. Because poor families still needed the income from their children more than they needed them to be educated, employed children who were under the age of 13 were obliged to have a certificate indicating that they had reached a certain level of education.

This was not always adhered to. In 1893 the school-leaving age was raised to 11 and then to 12 in 1899.

Various Parliamentary Acts followed which culminated in the system we have today. Today less than 1% of all adults in Britain are totally illiterate, although there are many who still struggle with reading despite the level of education now attainable.

2 - Education for the Disabled

Prior to the 1870s for the blind, the deaf and others with disabilities education was rare. A few charities had set up institutions particularly for the blind and deaf, but generally they were excluded from the system.

In 1874 the London School Board established a class for the deaf at a public elementary school and in 1875 it did the same for blind children. By 1888 there were 14 centres for the deaf and 23 centres for the blind attached to ordinary schools, catering for about 500 children. In 1875 the London Board made the first arrangements for teaching blind children in its elementary schools. A few other boards made provision for the deaf and blind, but it was the exception rather than the norm.

In 1893 the Elementary Education (Blind and Deaf Children) Act required school authorities (boards, district councils or school attendance committees) to make provision for the education of blind and deaf children resident in their area, who were not receiving suitable elementary education.

However, unlike the blind and deaf, other physically disabled and the mentally disabled children had no large organisations to fight their cause. After the 1870 Education Act these children were often incorporated into the normal elementary school system which caused problems.

The Royal Commission on the Blind and Deaf, who also covered other special needs, made a report in 1889 that made a distinction between 3 different levels of mental disability - the feeble-minded, imbeciles and idiots. It stated that the feeble-minded should receive special education separately from ordinary children, that imbeciles should attend institutions where they could and receive an education concentrating on sensory and physical development and the improvement of speech, and that idiots should be considered to be uneducable.

By 1896 there were 24 special schools in London attended by 900 pupils and by the end of the century schools for 'defective' children had been established by 6 other boards.

3 – Apprenticeships

Apprenticeships in England date back to medieval times when the craft guilds were established. Guilds were originally set up from the 10th century onwards when merchants formed alliances to band together for protection on their trading routes. From these merchant guilds the craft guilds developed, allowing tradesmen to set rules and restrictions within their own trade to protect standards and quality of craftsmanship. These guilds often relied on the apprenticeship system and people from the higher classes would sometimes send their children away to live with host families to learn a trade.

At first there were no strict rules or guidelines, but in 1563 the Statute of Artificers and Apprentices was passed. This regulated the system and forbade anyone to practise a trade without first having served a minimum of 7 years as an apprentice.

The Poor Relief Act of 1601 allowed authorities to bind a child to a master and apprenticeships began to be a way of instruction for more than just the wealthier classes. This was mostly to stop the child being a drain on the resources of the parish, which was often the case with illegitimate and orphaned children. At first children as young as 7 could be apprenticed. Most apprentices were boys, but some girls were accepted in trades such as seamstresses, bakers and stationers. At first the master was obliged to give the apprentice board, lodging and clothing, but little else. The child was originally bound until the age of 24, this being reduced to 21 in 1778. During this time the 'boys' were forbidden to marry. However, 'girls' could be released from their apprenticeships early if they married. After all a married woman was the responsibility of her husband and society was freed from any accountability for her financial and moral well being!

In 1747 William Hogarth made a series of engravings called "Industry and Idleness" which consisted of 12 plates depicting an industrious apprentice and an idle apprentice.

Overleaf are 4 of them. Each image included a verse from Proverbs in the Bible, which gives us an idea into how the work ethic and the importance of God played a big part in Georgian Britain.

"The Idle 'Prentice at Play in the Church Yard during Divine Service"

"The Industrious 'Prentice performing the duty of a Christian"

"The Idle 'Prentice Executed at Tyburn"

"The Industrious 'Prentice Lord-Mayor of London"

In 1801 a Parliamentary Act required that apprenticeship registers should be kept and in 1802, Peel's Factory Act was passed. It mainly dealt with the ill treatment of children in the ever increasing factory system, but it also considered the welfare of apprentices. Employers had to provide instruction in reading, writing and arithmetic during at least the first 4 years of the 7 years of apprenticeship and the hours that the apprentices could work were limited.

In 1814, the 1563 Statute was repealed and removed the 7 years minimum requirement.

Legislation continued to improve conditions, but even from the earliest and harshest forms of apprenticeship, it was still often a way that an otherwise poor and unskilled child could learn a trade that would put him or her very slightly above the very lowest members of society. Unfortunately, the practice by the parish of forcing children into apprenticeships to learn a trade was sometimes lax and the children were sent to farms, private homes or shops merely to become unpaid servants.

However, many were lucky enough to learn a trade and many spent time as a journeyman at the end of their term of apprenticeship. This meant they were still hired by the master craftsmen, but were paid a wage. Sometimes the journeymen went on to become master tradesmen themselves, but unfortunately others never did acquire their own workshop.

Compulsory apprenticeship was finally abolished in 1844, which coincided with the introduction of the Ragged schools, but even up until today it is still a useful way to learn a trade or occupation.

4 – Obtaining Information About Education and
   Apprenticeships

If you're trying to find where your ancestor was educated, Ancestry has a varied collection of school and university registers, in particular the London, England, School Admissions and Discharges, 1840-1911 which includes over 1 million pupils from 843 schools.

The 'National School Registers 1870 – 1914' on Find my Past, an example of which is below, covers (at the time of writing) 15,000 schools in 28 counties. Find my Past also has records of teachers from 1870 to 1948.

Below: sample record of a school register.

For records of Ragged Schools and other charitable organisations, it is more likely that you will find records (if they still exist) in the local archives or a trip to the National Archives might be useful.

For residential schools your first clue will often be in the censuses. If you have the name of the institution, then in my experience it is highly likely that you will find something online or in the local library about it.

Very recently my research took me to a boy who was, in 1871, a pupil at the Boy's Farm Home in East Barnet. By checking online I was able to establish that this was a part of the London Boys' Home initially founded in 1858 in Euston Road, London for destitute and wayward boys to teach them a trade. The Boy's Farm Home, as its names suggests, focussed on farm work. Unfortunately, none of the admission records still exist, so it was not possible to find under what circumstances he was admitted. However, he was a domestic gardener all his life and died in 1923 in a very pretty village in Sussex leaving an estate of £122 7s 11d (which is over £5000 in today's money).

Registers were kept from very early on with regard to the duties masters had to pay for apprentices that were not bound to them by the parish. The UK Register of Duties Paid for Apprentices' Indentures, 1710-1811 on Ancestry is an extremely useful tool (see below). However, if your ancestor was bound to a master by the parish, then it is more likely that, if the records still survive, they will be found in local archives. From 1836 they are also available at the National Archives in the 'Poor Law union indexes and papers'.

Ancestry also has Merchant Navy apprenticeship records, 'Articles of Clerkship' relating to contracts between an apprentice clerk and an attorney, and extracted apprenticeship records from West Yorkshire.

Find my Past has the registers of duties paid by masters under Britain, Country Apprentices 1710-1808' as well as several other useful catalogues containing apprenticeships including extracts from London, Dorset and Somerset and various London guild registers.

If your ancestor may have been apprenticed at one of London's livery companies, then a very useful site is www.londonroll.org.

Sometimes there would be disputes between apprentices and their masters and sometimes parents would simply refuse to let their children go. Records of these disagreements may be found in Parish Overseer's records in local archives if they have survived and you are lucky enough to find them.

Sometimes you find something out by chance. Recently I found a mention of an apprenticeship in a Last Will and Testament. Whilst I couldn't find a copy of the apprenticeship record itself, it did confirm by the trade that my research was going in the right direction.

As with most of your research, finding where your ancestor was (or *if* he or she was) educated or apprenticed, is partly hard work and partly luck.

****

Chapter 11 – Geographical Mobility and Population Growth

The further you go back with your research, the more likely it is that you will find that your ancestors stayed in the same place for generations. As previously pointed out, most people were poor and the Poor Laws would not allow the movement of people between towns and villages without documentation, so it was easier for most people to stay in the town or village where they were born.

Some people would have had trades, such as the blacksmiths and bakers and these trades would have been passed down from father to son. It is likely that they would have provided for the same town or village through generations. Most however, would have been casual labourers working on local farms and earning what they could when it was available. Agricultural work was seasonal and often poorly paid.

With the dawn of the Industrial Revolution, things began to change. New machinery on farms could do the work of a dozen men and many moved from the rural areas into the ever expanding towns and cities, their already precarious choice of living made even harder. Factory jobs employed men, women and children all year round, so despite the often squalid and cramped conditions of urban life, it was considered preferable to starvation. Consequently, the population movement within England became far more common.

"Over London" by Gustav Dore

Other factors that lured people to the towns and cities were the better chance of education for their children in Sunday Schools and the belief that the houses were better built.

As well as people moving within England, there also began to be more migration. This was sometimes due to the transportation of criminals, sometimes through necessity and sometimes through choice. There was a whole new world waiting for them across the oceans and many took a chance and ventured forth.

From the early 19th century the Irish had been coming to England and the USA, and the potato blight of the 1840s saw an estimated 1 million Irish leave their shores for a new life.

During the late 18th and into the middle of the 19th centuries the Scottish Land Clearances, which saw tenant farmers being forced from their homes, meant that the Scots too were forced to flee. Many emigrated to Australia, New Zealand or Canada, but some moved across the border to England.

Between 1700 and 1750, the population of England stayed relatively stable. Then, between 1750 and 1850, it more than doubled. This however, was not just due to the arrival of the Scots and Irish. Indeed during this time many English families were emigrating to the British Colonies themselves, which would, to a degree, have counteracted it.

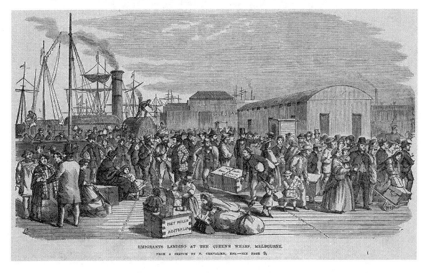

"Emigrants Landing at the Queen's Wharf Melbourne" by Nicholas Chevalier

In fact the combined population of England, Scotland, Ireland and Wales in 1801 was an estimated 18 million; by 1851 it was 27 million. The death rate was decreasing as children were more likely to survive infancy and as a better awareness of the need for sanitation grew, along with the introduction of some inoculations.

Another factor was that people were beginning to marry younger. With a more steady income it was easier for people to set up home together and earlier marriages meant more children. So there were simply more people being born than were dying. In 1700 an estimated 17% of the English population lived in urban areas, by 1801 this had increased to around 28% and by 1851 over half lived in the towns and cities. Of course one thing that made movement from one place to another much easier was the great advancements in transportation. With the building of the railways, a journey that would have taken days could be done in hours.

The Great Western Railway Terminus, at Paddington, London - Designed by I K Brunel and M D Wyatt from The Illustrated London news 8th July 1854.

Prior to the increase in geographical mobility following the Industrial Revolution, other factors played a part. For centuries religious belief had led to discrimination against both Protestants and Catholics depending on the monarch at any given time and in the early 18th century more than 50,000 French Protestants or Huguenots fled to our shores to escape their own persecution.

Whilst on the subject of religion, it is worth mentioning here that parish records for English Catholics are not the easiest to find online. Ancestry and Find My Past have a few, as does www.thegenealogist.co.uk but it is more likely that local research will be of further use on this subject although the websites www.catholic-history.org.uk and www.catholicfhs.wordpress.com may also be of some help.

If you are looking for Jewish ancestors, then there are a couple of very useful websites at www.jewishgen.org and www.jgsb.org.uk

To sum up, there has always been some mobility within, as well as to and from England, but prior to 1800, you are much more likely to have ancestors that stayed put.

If you can trace a surname back to the 1851 census where it first gives a place of birth, then there is a reasonable chance that you may have found the village or at least an adjoining village or town where your ancestors had lived for generations. Of course, as with any other research, take care. Forenames were not very varied and your line might have married and moved away, with a cousin with the same name still residing in the one you are looking at.

As mentioned before, villages and towns are not always within the same county or boundary over time. Make allowances for this. A good source for checking historical counties is 'Great Britain, Atlas and Index of Parish Registers' on Ancestry.

One last website worth mentioning if you want to know more about the places and times that your ancestors lived is www.british-history.ac.uk. Indeed this site has a wealth of information from primary and secondary sources relating to British history from 1300 onwards including maps and gazetteers and it can help to give you a real insight into the lives of those who came before.

****

Chapter 12 – Scotland & Ireland

1 – Scotland

Tracing your Scottish ancestors can be more difficult and more expensive than tracing those in England and Wales. This is mainly because almost all original online records are on the website www.scotlandspeople.gov.uk.

This site does not offer subscriptions, and although access to some of the indexes is free of charge, to actually look further and find out if the name you are looking at is the right one, you need to buy credits. Viewing each image can cost over £1 and there is no guarantee that you have found the right one meaning a lot of money wasted.

Of course if you live close enough to visit the National Records of Scotland facilities in Edinburgh, then you will have access to all the records without having to pay, except for a small charge for copies of documents. As with all records offices it is advisable to visit their website first and register as a user. The website, www.nrscotland.gov.uk, also gives lots of information on what is available and how to find it.

"Edinburgh Castle and the Grassmarket from Candlemaker Row" by Henry G. Duguid

The first time I undertook Scottish research was for a client with ancestors in the Highlands and as I live on the south coast of England, visiting the archives would have proved very costly. However, after finding that I was spending a lot of my client's money on the Scotland's People website, I subscribed to the Highland Family History Society at:

www.highlandfamilyhistorysociety.org.

I emailed them regarding my particular needs, and the treasurer John Durham very kindly telephoned me and gave me some very useful advice. He put me in touch with a society member, Mrs Margaret Mackay who visits the Edinburgh Archives regularly and carries out research for clients at a very reasonable rate. She has been a godsend enabling me to save my clients' money and removing the frustration of paying for several wrong document images, before (if lucky) finding the correct one. This is often the case because there are far less surnames in Scotland than in England and Wales, so if you are searching for a Donald Mackenzie and know little else about them, the chances of you stumbling across the right one straight away are quite small.

I am very keen on using family history societies and they are well worth checking out. As I have mentioned before they can be a very useful tool to varying degrees and they all offer different services, but in my experience the good ones have provided a wealth of help and information. The Scottish Association of Family History Societies at www.safhs.org.uk provides a comprehensive list.

If you are content with transcripts, rather than images of original documents (bearing in mind the possible inaccuracies through human error), then there are Scottish birth, marriage and death records and census records on Ancestry and www.familysearch.org. Find My Past also has transcripts of the censuses and a limited amount of birth, marriage and death records. Ancestry holds some other original documentation, so if you check through all the displayed records for your ancestor, you may come across something unexpected such as their time working on a trade ship or their school admission dates.

Like England and Wales the censuses began in 1841 and give the same information. Some later censuses give extras like how many windows a dwelling had and whether the individual spoke Gaelic or Gaelic and English, all snippets that give a more rounded picture of your ancestor. The transcripts are available up until 1901 on Ancestry and Find My Past. To find a 1911 census it is once again a matter of going to the Scotland's People website and buying credits or visiting the National or Local Archives. Again, you may be lucky and find someone who can do this for you.

The official registers of birth, marriage and death were not introduced in Scotland until 1855. The good news is that if you are able to find them then they give a much wider amount of information that those of England and Wales. As well as all the information you can find on England and Wales certificates, the Scottish birth and death records give an actual time of the event and the mother's maiden name (preceded by M S). The birth records also give a date and place of the parent's marriage and the death records give the marital status of the deceased. The marriage records give the names of the couple's mothers and their maiden names. All of these 'extras' can help to confirm that you have the right person. Above and overleaf are examples of post 1855 birth, marriage and death records.

Example 2.

The bad news is that prior to 1855, parish registers for the Church of Scotland were not kept nearly as fastidiously as those in England and Wales. It is possible to trace families back a long way, but it is really a matter of luck. Again, as Scottish names are less varied even if you find a record, there is usually only a sparse amount of information available, so no guarantee that you have the right one. A particularly good resource for finding where these records are available is the National Library of Scotland website at www.nls.uk.

If you are searching for Catholic ancestors, then the Scottish Catholic Archives in Edinburgh:

(www.scottishcatholicarchives.org.uk) will give you an indication as to what is available and where.

Another very useful place to visit when tracing your Scottish ancestors is the Scottish Genealogy Society which is also based in Edinburgh. Their website is www.scotsgenealogy.com and it has a lot of information on where records can be obtained.

One final online destination that I would like to mention here is http://edina.ac.uk/stat-acc-scot which has the statistical accounts for Scotland from 1791 to 1845. It has very detailed descriptions of many Scottish towns which put real flesh on the bones of your ancestors. Sites like this and www.british-history.ac.uk provide information that is every bit as important in my work as finding names and dates. It brings a whole new aspect to family history research and I thoroughly recommend it.

2 – Ireland

"A Boating Party in Cork Harbour" by George Mounsey 1840

Researching Irish ancestry can bring about its own problems. Between 1800 and 1922 Ireland was a part of the UK. During the Civil War in 1922 the Public Record Office was burned down and many historical documents were destroyed including census returns, Church of Ireland parish registers and wills and testamentary records. However, it is not all bad news. Some records did survive and many records and transcripts were not housed in the Public Records Office.

There is actually still a wealth of information out there and many websites that can aid genealogical research. The following list covers those I recommend. Remember that this list is not exhaustive and a little time spent googling occasionally brings up surprising information. To get you started though (and they may well be all you need), the following websites are extremely informative:

www.ancestry.co.uk (click on the Card Catalogue and then click on Ireland)

www.findmypast.com (click on the A-Z of Record Collections and then click on Ireland)

www.irish-genealogy-toolkit.com

www.nli.ie *The National Library of Ireland*

www.theirisharchives.com *The Irish Archives*

www.ancestryireland.com *Ulster Historical Foundation*

www.celticcousins.net

www.nifhs.org *The Northern Ireland Family History Group*

www.familyhistory.ie *The Genealogical Society of Ireland (Irish Republic)*

www.ifhs.ie *Irish Family History Society (Irish Republic)*

www.proni.gov.uk *The Public Record Office of Northern Ireland*

www.nationalarchives.ie *The National Archives of Ireland*

The latter 2 are the main public records offices if you plan on visiting the archives in person. They are to be found in Belfast and Dublin respectively.

****

In Conclusion

Hopefully by now you have begun your research and have discovered some interesting information about your ancestors. Perhaps shocking, perhaps surprisingly comforting, but almost certainly fascinating.

Don't forget to periodically return to any unsolved mysteries and check again on your favourite websites. Subscribe to the newsletters on these sites, as they often send updates on new collections. Look out for new websites that may hold more information and don't be afraid to email organisations or individuals who may have more detailed knowledge of your ancestors. You may get no response or you may get the answer to that all important question that has been holding up your research.

One final thing –

This is a journey. Don't anticipate the destination, just enjoy the ride!

****

Bibliography

Fowler, Simon, *Workhouse,* Kew, 2007

Hart-Davis, Adam, *What the Victorians Did for Us,* Headline Book Publishing, 2001

May, Trevor, *An Economic and Social History of Britain 1760–1970,* Longman Group, 1987
roger spro
Middleton, Haydn, *People in the Past – Tudor Rich and Poor,* Harcourt Education, 2003

Murray, Peter, *Access to History - Poverty and Welfare,* Oxon, 1999

Pritchard, R.E., *Dickens's England – Life in Victorian Times,* The History Press, 2002, 2009

Strange, K. H., *The Climbing Boys - A Study of Sweeps Apprentices 1773-1875,* London, 1982

Wise, Sarah, *The Blackest Streets - The Life and Death of a Victorian Slum,* London, 2008

Gillard D (2011) *Education in England: a briefhistory/*www.educationengland.org.uk

https://en.wikipedia.org/wiki/History_of_the_British_Army
https://en.wikipedia.org/wiki/History of the Royal Air Force
https://en.wikipedia.org/wiki/History of the Royal Navy
www.bbc.co.uk/history
www.bl.uk/victorian-britain

www.britainexpress.com/History
www.british-history.ac.uk
www.census-helper.co.uk
www.commonslibraryblog.com
www.educationengland.org.uk
www.hierarchystructure.com
www.historyextra.com
www.historyhouse.co.uk
www.historylearningsite.co.uk
www.historytoday.com
www.historicengland,org.uk
www.localhistories.org
www.medieval-life-and-times.info
www.navycs.com/uk
www.oxford-royale.co.uk
www.raf.mod.uk
www.shakespeare-online.com
www.timeref.com
www.trainingzone.co.uk

****

INDEX

Domestic servants, 58
Dr Barnardos, 23

East Sussex Records Office, 15
Education, 7, 101, 105, 110
Edward VI, 37
Elizabeth 1st, 37
Empire, 64
English Civil War, 37, 96
Enumeration Districts, 31

Family History Societies, 15, 122
Feudal system, 52
Find my Past, 12, 20, 25, 29, 30, 31, 40, 61, 69, 75, 85, 111, 113
First World War, 67, 68, 70, 95

Gentry, 36, 53
Geographical Mobility, 7, 114
Government Record Office, 20
Great Fire of London, 90

Hardwicke's Marriage Act, 39
Husbandmen, 53

Industrial Revolution, 6, 43, 60, 92, 115, 118
Infant mortality rates, 96
Internet, 5, 12
Ireland, 7, 20, 23, 28, 65, 82, 87, 90, 117, 120, 125, 126, 127
Isle of Man, 28

Jewish ancestors, 118
Jews, 39

Kelly's Directories, 61

PAULINE GOLDS
www.bygonelives.com

Pauline Golds is a genealogist and writer living on the south coast of England. Previous literary works consist of a nostalgic stroll through her childhood in 1960s Sussex, as well as an historical novel inspired by a wealth of colourful discoveries made about her ancestors through tracing her own family tree.

From Greyscale to Technicolour and *Silhouettes in a Silent Land* are available to preview and purchase at www.paulinegolds.com

In her role as a genealogist, Pauline's aim is to give an affordable service to those on a budget. If you are interested in learning more about having research carried out for you or have any questions relating to tracing your own family tree please visit www.bygonelives.com or email pauline@bygonelives.com

Other titles in The Emerald Series

Emerald Publishing produces a range of titles covering a variety of areas. if you would like to get more information on our titles please go to www,emeraldpublishing.co.uk